THE
FAMILY FOREST

BY

MARGARET M. RUSSELL

ULPHA PRESS

First published in Great Britain in 2000
by Ulpha Press
32 Granada Road, Denton, Manchester M34 2LJ

ISBN 0-9538973-0-3

Designed and typeset by M. & D. Slater

Printed and bound by Woolnough Bookbinders Ltd.
Irthlingborough, Northamptonshire.

Cover photograph:
'The Oaks', Loughrigg.

*This book is dedicated to the
memory of my parents,
Herbert Casson and Edith Margaret Hird*

CONTENTS

Part 4. Cassons

Part 5. Miscellanea

ACKNOWLEDGEMENTS

The following have kindly given permission for me to reproduce excerpts from their estate papers:-

Lord Egremont for the Leaconfield Papers;
Mrs. Gordon Duff-Pennington for the Pennington Papers;
The Cumbria County Archivist for the Rydal Papers;
and Lord Lonsdale for the Lowther family archives. These archives are the property of the Lowther family trustees, with whom the copyright resides.

Colin Baxter Photography has given permission to reproduce the photograph of Stickle Tarn on page 16.

I should also like to thank the many people who have given me help and encouragement over the years, especially the following, many of whom have given me access to family letters and papers and loaned me photographs with permission for their use in this book:-
Janet Arnison, Eddie Casson, Steve Foster, Barbary Greenhow, the late C. Roy Huddleston, the late Fred Hughes, Anne Kirkby, Jean Lincoln, Bob Mandell, the late John Porter, Reg Postlethwaite, the late Dr. W. Rollinson, Joan Shrewsbury, Derek and Mary Slater and Audrey Sykes. To Jim Gristenthwaite, Cumbria County Archivist and the staffs of all four Record Offices, both past and present, for their untiring help. To the staff of the Lancashire Record Office in Preston. To Stella Colwell for reading the text and writing the foreword, and finally to the two people who insisted that I finished the work, one is Peter Park, the other wishes to remain anonymous. To you all - thankyou.

I also acknowledge with gratitude, the assistance of the Curwen Archives Trust.

FOREWORD

When Margaret Russell asked me if I would write a foreword to her book, I didn't realise how many of her ancestral families (and I do mean *many* families) had passed through the records of my own parish of Grasmere. For forty years Margaret has patiently and relentlessly pursued the Hirds, Batemans, Tysons, Stephensons, Viccars, Dawsons, Jacksons, Sherwens, Moores, Nicholsons, Cassons and others, over the lakeland fells along the packhorse routes from their homes in the Duddon Valley. Hers is a truly Cumbrian background, but its branches can be traced to Australia, New Zealand, Canada and America.

Margaret travelled mainly by public transport to Cumbrian and Lancashire record offices in search of her heritage, and what a wealth of information she has discovered! The numerous wills reveal people who were generous to their family, making them a genealogical goldmine; the probate inventories show that they did not squander their money, their possessions and farm stock display a high degree of domestic comfort, and moneys owed to them the extent to which they supported their neighbours. Margaret has found one or two 'characters' in her family tree, but as we all know, 'there's nowt as queer as folk'.

This book is full of little gems, and for anyone in these families or with Lake District roots, this forest of cousins Margaret has so lovingly uncovered will prove of lasting value.

Stella Colwell,
Polstead,
Suffolk.
2000.

INTRODUCTION

When my children no longer needed my care and attention, I decided to compile the 'Family Tree'. Now, almost forty years later, I know one can never achieve this, so there comes a time when it is advisable to write up what has been discovered. I have had much pleasure unravelling the mysteries of my ancestors, how they lived, loved and died but, instead of a 'Tree' I have ended up with a 'Forest' - hence the title of this narrative.

Over the time that I have been researching, I have met hundreds of people, visited Record Offices and found many cousins, the degree does not matter, the important thing is that you all have the same roots. It is a hobby I can recommend as, through it, I have made friends throughout the U.K. and overseas.

Once written, the hard work began and this is when my kinsfolk, Mary and Derek Slater took over. They have edited the manuscript, designed the page layout, arranged the illustrations, drawn the maps, produced the 'names' index, taken some of the photographs and designed the cover. I am greatly indebted to them as, without their help this book would never have been published. Thank you both.

I have cross-checked the material I have used wherever possible, but even so, there may be errors for which I am entirely responsible. My advice to everyone researching their family history, is always to check everything yourself - a lesson that I learned the hard way!

Margaret M. Russell
Denton, Manchester.
April, 2000

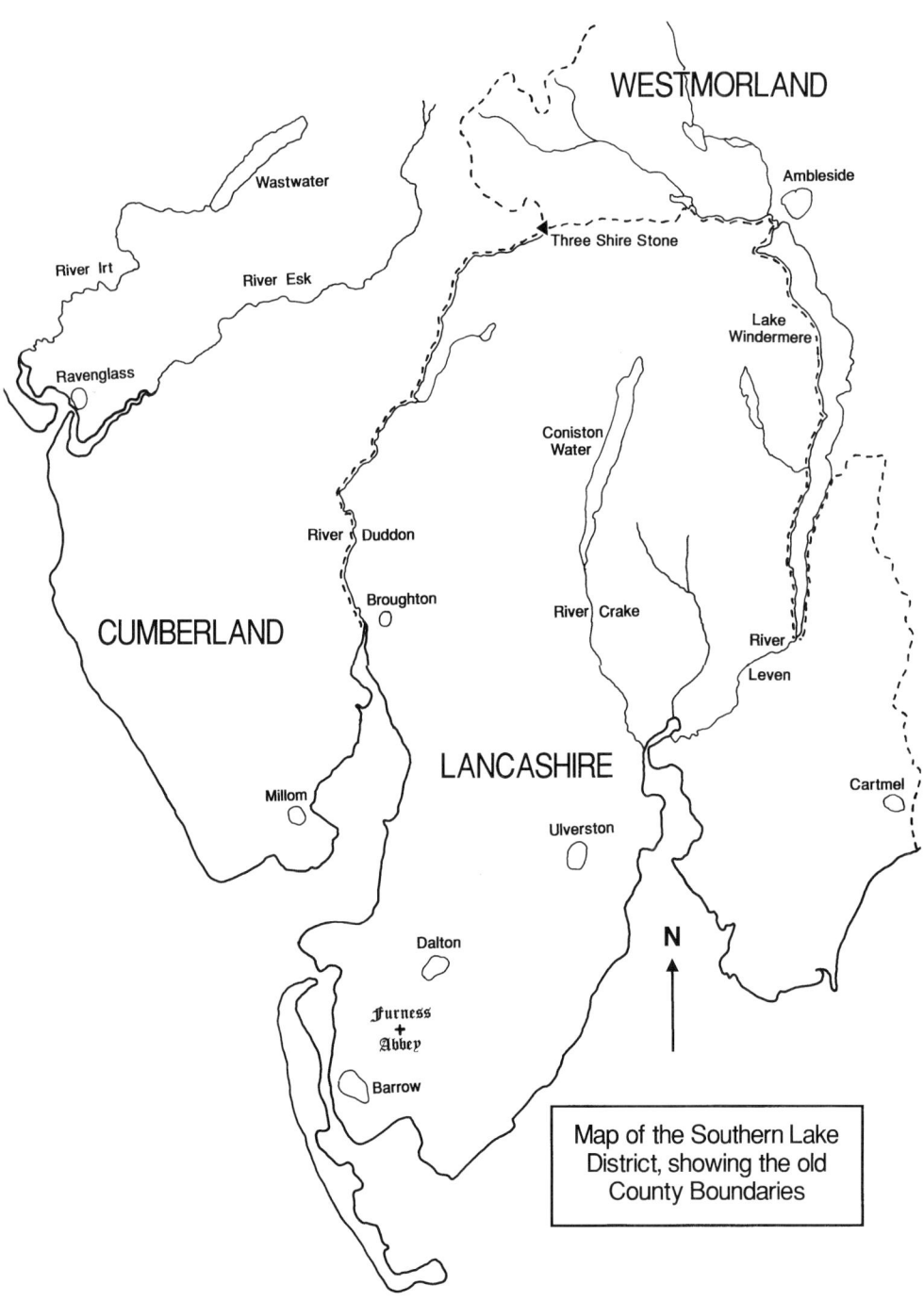

WESTMORLAND

Wastwater

River Irt

River Esk

Ambleside

Three Shire Stone

Lake Windermere

Ravenglass

Coniston Water

River Duddon

CUMBERLAND

Broughton

River Crake

River Leven

LANCASHIRE

Millom

Cartmel

Ulverston

Dalton

N

Furness + Abbey

Barrow

Map of the Southern Lake District, showing the old County Boundaries

HIRD ANCESTORS

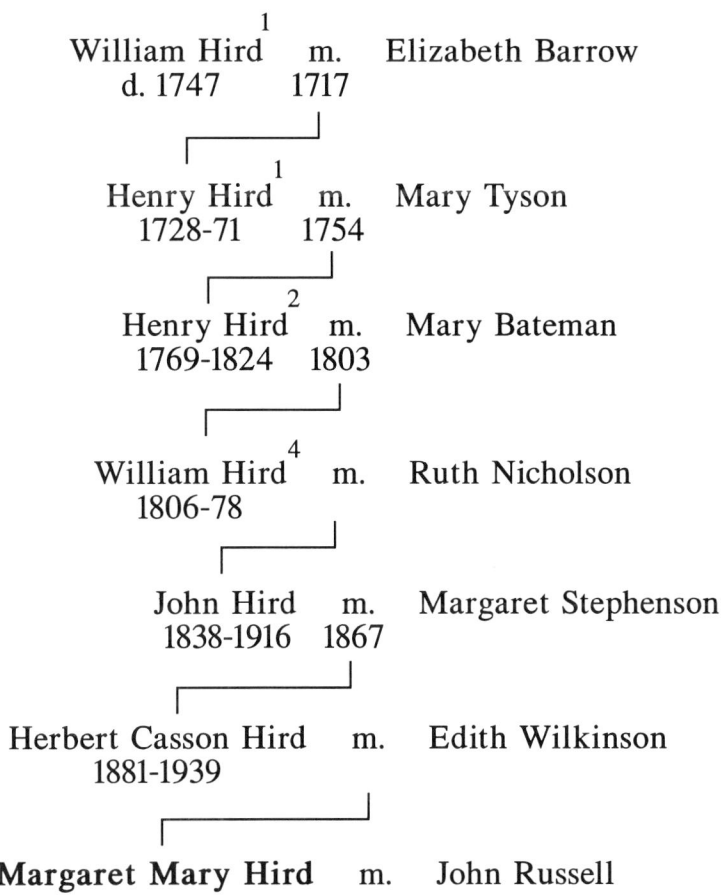

William Hird[1] m. Elizabeth Barrow
d. 1747 1717

Henry Hird[1] m. Mary Tyson
1728-71 1754

Henry Hird[2] m. Mary Bateman
1769-1824 1803

William Hird[4] m. Ruth Nicholson
1806-78

John Hird m. Margaret Stephenson
1838-1916 1867

Herbert Casson Hird m. Edith Wilkinson
1881-1939

Margaret Mary Hird m. John Russell

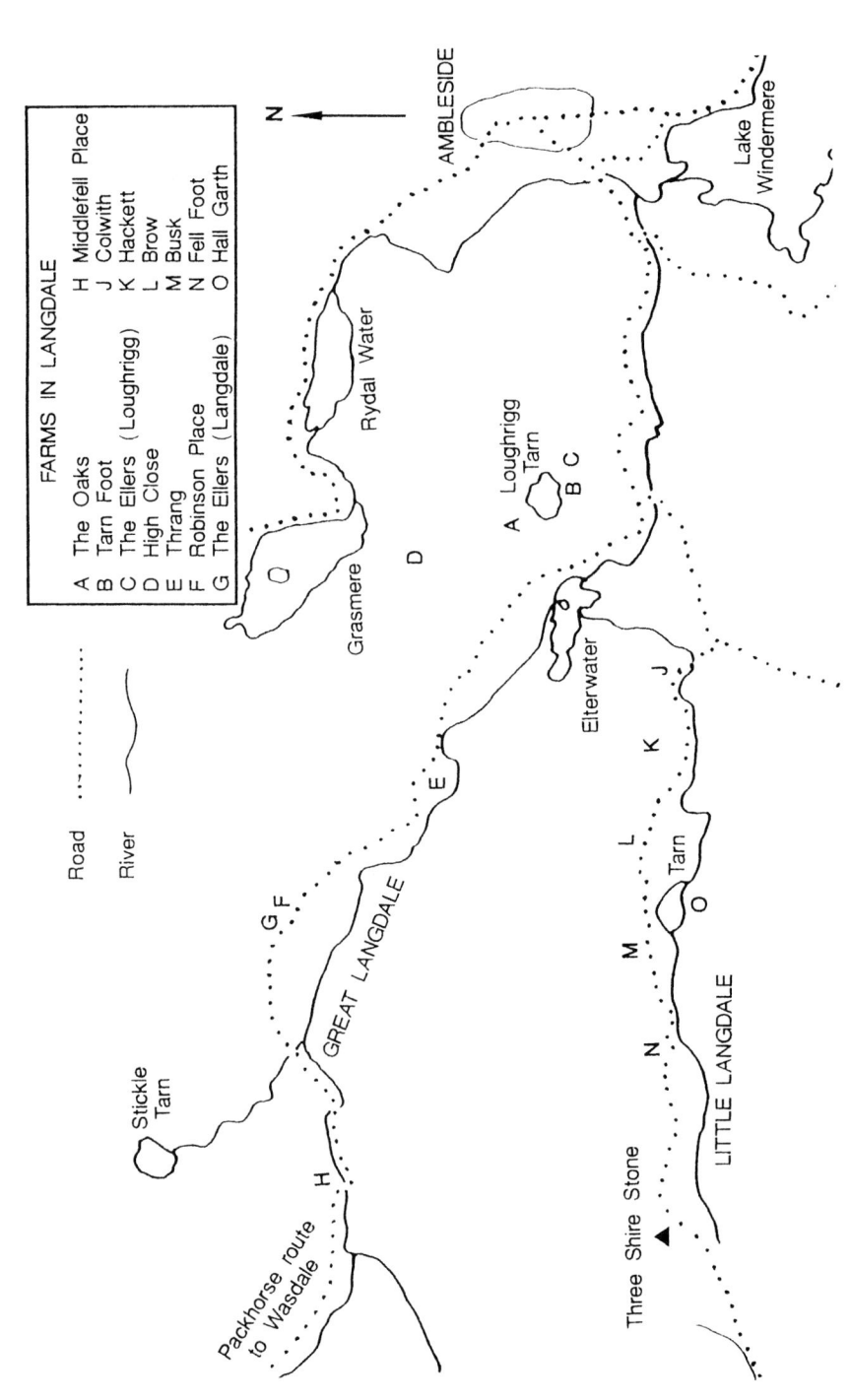

FARMS IN LANGDALE

A The Oaks H Middlefell Place
B Tarn Foot J Colwith
C The Ellers (Loughrigg) K Hackett
D High Close L Brow
E Thrang M Busk
F Robinson Place N Fell Foot
G The Ellers (Langdale) O Hall Garth

Road ·········
River ⌇

N

AMBLESIDE

Lake Windermere

Rydal Water

Loughrigg Tarn

A
B C

Grasmere

D

Elterwater

E

J

K

GREAT LANGDALE

L
Tarn
O

G F

M

N

H

Stickle Tarn

Packhorse route to Wasdale

Three Shire Stone

LITTLE LANGDALE

PART 1 - THE HIRDS

Early information

The Cumberland Lay Subsidy, 6th year of Edward lll (1332) refers to:-

> *Thomas le Hird, Brugh;*
> *John le Hird, Beauant;*
> *Julian le Hird, Wyggeton* (Wigton);
> *Ivo of Blackhale;*
> *John of Aykton;*
> *Adam & John of Boulton;*
> *Thomas & Thomas son of Thomas, of Dalston.*

I do not know whether or not any of these migrated to found the Westmorland families, but Hirds were established in Grasmere in 1560 when they are mentioned in the Court Roll, Oliver and John each paying 2d for Greenhow.

There were also Hirds living in West Cumberland in the early 17c using the same Christian names - John, William, Thomas, Henry etc., but I have not been able to link them with my family from Grasmere. There are still some there, some were also in the Cartmel area and some in Yorkshire.

By the late 16c. they were well established in Grasmere, the first recorded baptism is:-

30th March 1571, Elizabeth, daughter of Robert Hird.

This is followed over the next few years by children of Michael, Christopher, John, William and Edward. William, son of John Hird was buried 29th November 1572 and in September 1571, Christopher Hird married Elizabeth Watson.

Amongst the Lonsdale Archives at Carlisle, I recently came across a rather unusual Hearth Tax for Grasmere dated 1683 which, as well as the number of hearths in a household, also gave the number of inhabitants, their ages and, for most of the adults, their status. Hirds listed are as follows:-

John Hird widdower (sic), in the same house the *males, 40, 3, 6, and 6 mths & females 26, 17 & 2.* No hearths recorded, maybe they did not have one.

Wm. Hird, husbandman, 53, 26. His wife 55, 18. They had one hearth
and I am presuming the 26 and 18 year olds were children.
Edward Hird, waller, 45, 5. Wife 38, 7, 1, 85, 40, 34, 30. A very varied
household with just one hearth.
Robert Hird, widdower, 56, 21. Females 83, 22. Was the 83 year old
his mother?
Wm.Hird, husbandman, 40, 20, 15, 11, 2, his wife 45, 8, 5 & 5. Were
these twins? Again one hearth.

Almost a hundred years later, in 1777 when the Window Tax was
collected, there was only a single family of that name - Robert Hird
living in Grasmere. Where had they all gone? Over and over again,
wonderful information but tantalising, as one can only guess the relationships.

From some of these I am descended, but I have only proof of the
line from William[1] Hird, shoemaker, who, in 1717, married Elizabeth
Barrow of the Oaks, Loughrigg at Grasmere Church.

Grasmere in 1780 (from West - *'Guide to the Lakes'*)

Hirds in Grasmere and Loughrigg

William[1] and Elizabeth went to live at the Oaks, which eventually belonged to their descendants, or to High Close which was also in the Hird Family. They produced five children.

From reading various wills with their mention of cousins, I think, but have no definite proof, that the William[1] above had the following siblings.

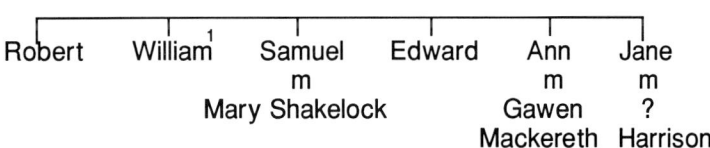

Robert	William[1]	Samuel	Edward	Ann	Jane
		m		m	m
		Mary Shakelock		Gawen	?
				Mackereth	Harrison

In 1747, a Robert Hird of Gillside died. His will, proved on the 18th of May that year, had been made it ten years earlier. He mentions *John, William and Thomas my three sons* and *Anne & Agnes my two daughters*, all to receive Twenty pounds apiece to be *paid forth of my Customary Estate at Gillside by Robert Hird my son and Heir Aparient when he shall Attain the Age of Twenty one Years*. His wife was Mary. This could be the above Robert.

In 1765 Samuel's son John died. In his will he mentions his *'customary Messuage and Tenement at Tarnfoot in Loughrigg* and *his dales and Peatmoss lying and being at Oxenfell in the Bayliffwick of Hawkshead.'* He left money to support his father Samuel and his mother Mary and to his nephew Robert Brockbank *'my fooling (fowling) gun'*. He made his cousin, George Mackereth, his executor. The residue went to his two sisters, but no names are mentioned.

John, the eldest son of William[1] and Elizabeth, married Sarah ? and went eventually to live at Fell Foot, Little Langdale. He is recorded as paying 4s.2d Window Tax in 1777; there is also a Thomas Hird who paid 3s.0d. John had two sons, John and James and four daghters - Elizabeth, Sarah, Mary and Anne. Although I have information about these families and am in touch with some descendants, I have not sufficient proof of the lineage to put it in print.

William[1] died in 1747, his will read as follows, after the preamble of his soul etc.

'.... and as for my Temporal Estate I dispose of as followeth, That is to say I give unto Elizabeth Hird my Dear and Loving Wife one half of

All my household goods Also I give unto John Hird my son my Best Coat Also I give unto William Hird my son my Cloaths Chest Also I give unto Henry Hird my son my Clock & Case Also I give unto Jane my daughter wife of William Dawson one stone of Fleece Wool Also I give unto Isabel my daughter one little Chest standing in the Parlour And All the residue of my Goods Credditts and Chattells I give unto Elizabeth my wife and and the said John William and Henry my sons and the said Jane and Isabel my daughters equally among them and I make the said Elizabeth my wife and John, William & Henry my sons and the said Jane and Isabel my daughters Joynt Executors they paying all my just debts and Funeral Expences And I doo hereby Revoke Disannull and make void all former and other Wills and testaments by me heretofore made and likewise declare this only to be my Last Will and testament whereof I the said William Hird the testator have hereunto sett my hand and seal the day and year First above written'

He made his mark and stamped it with his seal in the presence of the Witnesses:-
William Barrow
Samuel Hird
John Sawrey.

It was proved the *'8ᵗʰ day of February One thousand Seven Hundred and forty seven by Elizabeth Hird widow, William & Henry Hird Husbandmen & Isabel Hird spinster, all of Loughrigg and John Hird of Brathy in the parish of Hawkshead, Husbandman and power was reserved for Jane'* (whose surname on this bond is given as Danson not Dawson as in the will.)

Of the five, Henry and John signed their names.
The fact that Samuel Hird was witness to William's mark also suggests that he was his brother.

The Inventory is also of interest. It was taken on *'14ᵗʰ day of October in the year of our Lord one thousand seven hundred and forty seven by Edward Benson, John Mackereth, William Barrow and Thomas Roberts'* who all signed their names.

	£	s	d
Purse and apparel	4	0	0
Bedding and Bedstocks		15	0
Brass and Pewter		5	0
Earthen Vessels		7	0
Iron Potts, Pans etc.		5	0
Chests and Chairs		10	0
Clock and Case	2	0	0
(inventory torn)		1	0
... Wheels and Cards	2	15	0
Meal and Malt	1	1	0
Husbandry Gear		10	0
Horses and Furniture	5	15	0
Hay and Corn	5	0	0
Beasts	18	0	0
Money owing Deceased	3	15	2
	£ 44	19	2
Debitory	£ 29	0	0
Clear Total	£ 15	0	2

Of interest to me is the clock and case in the inventory.

Robert of Gillside had one, also valued at £2 and when Henry's youngest son died in 1771 he had clocks to the value of £4.17s., yet, despite years of research I have not been able to establish that the Hirds were clockmakers prior to Henry[3] of Thornhill, Dumfries, in the next century.

The Barrows

A little about Elizabeth's family. The Barrows cannot go unmentioned, because they are also my ancestors. They were in the parish of Grasmere in 1630 when, on 14th May, Henry Barrow, son of Henry of Loughrigg, was baptised. The late Dr. T. Fahy of Kendal, an authority on many Westmorland families, told me he was sure they came from the Cartmel/Flookburgh area, but I have not been able to prove this with certainty.

William, son of Henry Barrow, was baptised the following year; the young Henry, mentioned above, having died when only a few weeks old, a second Henry was baptised. Then, on 25th February 1640 the Register reads:-

'John Barrow son of Henry of the Oaks in Loughrigg'

This confirms their address. Henry was buried on 23rd September 1666 and from his will it would appear that only three of his children reached aduldhood.

I have reconstructed his family thus:

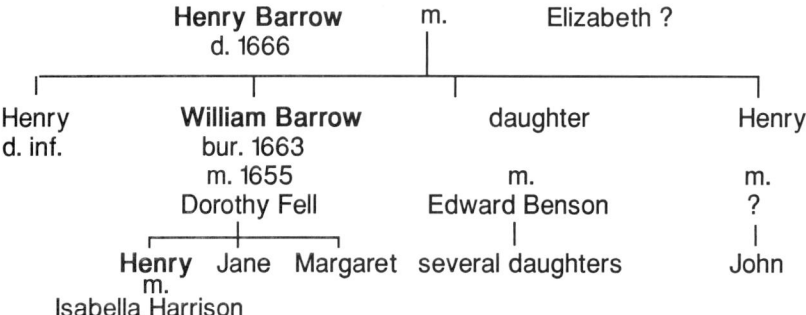

William Barrow, the eldest son, had predeceased his father leaving a young son, Henry, who was Heir at Law to the Oaks.

His grandfather appointed four trustees to look after the welfare of young Henry and his sisters until they reached the age of one and twenty. One of these was Reginald Brathwaitt of Loughrigg, another John Simpson of Flookburgh, in the county of Lancaster, which substantiates Dr. Fahy's theory of where the Barrow Family came from; the third trustee, Robert Braithwaite, also came from the same place. Henry Barrow, Henry's youngest son, was the fourth trustee and his address was given as Braithwaite, Cumberland. Information like this helps both Family and Social Historians. Apart from relationships, one realises the distances that executors, trustees, and supervisors had to travel to carry out their duties.

Grandfather Henry left goods and chattels to the value of £181.19.1d, so he was a wealthy man. The fact that he signed his will with a mark does not necessarily signify that he was illiterate. One must always remember that very few people made their wills until they were on their death beds. Education was an important matter in the lives of the yeomanry and Henry was no exception, stressing that his grandson should be educated.

Young Henry's uncle, Henry Barrow of Braithwaite, continued to live there until 1680 when he appointed Thomas Stranger of Cockermouth his attorney

'... to surrender give and yeald up for him and in his name into the hands of the Lord or Lords of the Manor of Braithwaite and Cowedell all the Closes, parcels of ground Called and Known by the name of Roughground Wallmill Closes and Collons with their and every of their appurtenances of the Yearly Customary rent of five shillings, situated at Great Braithwaite aforesaid to the only use and behalf of John Wilkinson of Thornthwaite.' (Ref.D/LEC/37 C.R.O. Carlisle)

The young Henry Barrow married Isabella Harrison bringing another name to research.

C17 Rushlight Holders

The Harrisons

What little I have found about the Harrisons has been obtained mostly from wills; once again, we find names occurring as witnesses or executors of our ancestors wills.

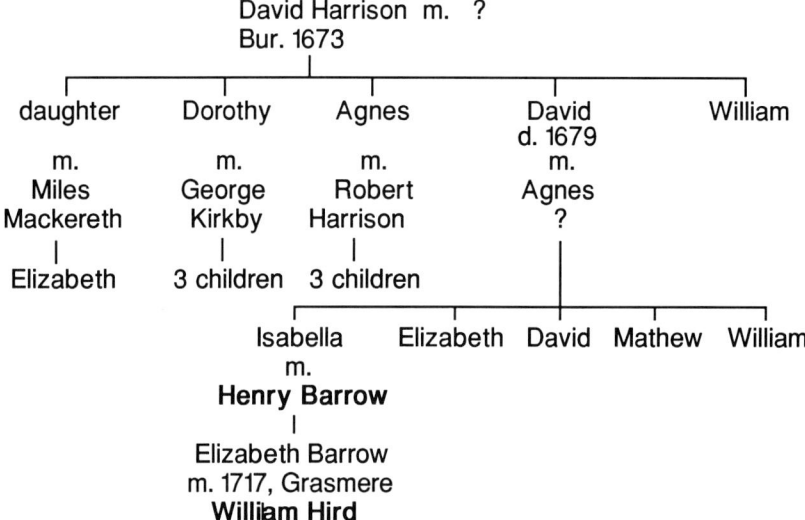

The Harrisons were from Rydal and the above tree was compiled from David's (bur 1673/4) will. The format of most wills are a set pattern, praising God for the testators perfect mind and memory, asking forgiveness for all their sins and requesting that their bodies be decently buried, but this one is just a bit different:-

*I give my soul into the hands of God who gave it and My body to the earth from whence it came to be buried In Xtian & decent manner in the parish Churchyard of Grasmere **Not doubting that at the General Resurection I shall receive the same again.***

This is the only time I have seen the last clause

His daughter, who married Miles Mackereth, must have predeceased him as she is not mentioned among the legatees, neither is Miles, but their daughter, Elizabeth, was left fourteen pounds. Both his other sons-in-law benefitted; George Kirkby received eight pounds and Robert Harrison twelve. His daughters, Dorothy and Agnes, each received nine stones of wool and his daughter-in-law, Agnes, wife of son David, got seven stones. His younger son, William, received 20s. He remembered all his grandchildren, but with the exception of David's children and Elizabeth Mackereth, he did not name them.

He must have been a thoughtful and generous man as he left *'to Elizabeth Robinson, now servant to my son David five shillings and to John Dawson another servant to son David half a crown.'* His estate was appraised at £84.4.5d. He owed £12.13.4d. and his funeral expenses were £7, so he must have had a good send off!

Young David died in 1679, just six years after his father. His will refers to only three children, so we must assume that Mathew and William had died. He refers to lands and tenements in Great Langdale:

'My lands or Tenement beyond the Beck commonly called Grigg Tenement of the annual Rent of six Pounds Also All that my Messuage or Tenement at Rossett and all my other Tenements or Farmholds of the Lands & Inheritance of Daniel Fleming Esq., of Rydal.'

This David was a rich man, his goods and chattels, appraised by Thomas Benson, George Kirkby, Robert Harrison and Anthony Atkinson, were valued at £210.12s., the most valuable items being the beasts and sheep.

His daughter, Isabella married Henry Barrow two years after her father's death.

Social History of this Period.

Local events which occurred at this period of time are not easily come by, but thanks to Sir Daniel Fleming, one of *His Majesties Justicies of ye Peace for the County of Westmorland*, we are able to piece together one or two things and build a picture.

Some readers may not be familiar with Sir Daniel Fleming of Rydal, despite his being well documented. He was born 1633, knighted 1681 and died in 1701. He was a scholar, antiquary, magistrate and meticulous recorder of events, estate matters and his work as a Justice of the Peace. His papers are deposited in the County Record Office, Kendal for all to study. His hand writing is extremely small. His Memoirs make very good reading, especially his advice to his son:

'Bring thy children up in Learning & Obedience yet without Austerity: praise them openly, and reprehend them secretly. Give them good countenance and convenient Maintenance according to thine ability, otherwise thy life will seem their Bondage, and then what Portions thou shall leave them at thy Death, they will thank Death for and not thee':

'Marry thy daughters in time lest they marry themselves'

Sir Daniel lived at Rydal Hall, from the reign of Charles 1st, through the Commonwealth, and the reigns of James 2nd and William and Mary. They were turbulent times. One tends to think that everything would be quite peaceful in Westmorland, but not so. Sir Daniel had to deal with various religious groups including the Quakers who were strong in the area. He issued many warrants for taking their goods to pay tithes and for holding meetings. A typical example is this one, issued for a meeting at the house of William Rawes in Langdale in 1684, when goods were taken from:-

William Rawes, Corn Cattle and Household Goods	£14 0	0
John Dixon, Beasts, Hat and Wool	£20 12	0
Michael Wilson, Goods worth	£ 12	6
Thomas Harrison, Wool worth	£ 13	6
John Walker, four Oxen and an Iron Pot	£16 8	0
James Harrison, Goods worth	£ 1 0	0
Dorothy Wilson & Rebecca, her Daughter	£ 1 14	0
John Rigg, Wool worth	£ 1 6	6
	£56 6	*6*

A lot of money, far in excess of the tithes.

A Robert Barrow, who lived in the district, was frequently being prosecuted, *(Besse's Sufferings, The Society of Friends, Friends House, London)*, but I do not know if he was a kinsman.

Sir Daniel had also to deal with highwaymen, coiners and at least one murder. I am grateful to Mr. Clarence Postlethwaite for sending me an enlarged script of the case, which saved me poring over the small writing. It concerns the brutal killing of one William Dixon of Millfell-place.

On 14th of July 1662, Daniel Fleming Esq. sent Greetings to the Constable of Langdale and commanded that *'upon Thursday next by ten of ye clock you bring before mee* (sic) *unto my house at Rydall the several persons here under written (and all others who may bee* (sic) *material witnesses) to inform mee on ye behalfe of our Sovereign Lord ye King concerning ye late death of William Dixon of the Millfell-place within your Constablewick. And fail not herein at your perill.'*

The following are the persons he had to make sure were there

Catherine Dixon	*Reginald Millfell*
Agnes Dixon	*Jo: Harrison*
Isabell Dixon	*Jo: Grigg*
Isabell Harrison	*Tho. Dixon*
Robert Harrison	*Ro. Satterthwaite*
Will. Harrison	*Jo: Johnston*
John Otlay	*Edward Benson of the High-close*
Charles Middlefell	*Jo: Stainton*

The village constable was appointed yearly at the Manor Court; this was one of the least popular jobs as it took so much of the farmer's time away from his tenement. I feel sure that the constable receiving this command would do some muttering under his breath as he would be called away during haytime.

Here are some of the statements.

'The murder was commited upon the 13th day of April last past according to the examination of Catherine Dixon upon oath who sayeth that William Dixon her late father upon the 13th. day of April last past about ye sunsetting told her he would go that night a fishing unto a place called Stickle Tarne, as he had formerly used to do and ye next morning about ye sunrising she went to look for her said father, whom she found lying dead in a place of ye fell called ye slaughter, with three wounds in his head and a bruise upon his right

hand, his tongue thrust forth of his mouth, and his teeth fastened upon it, his long beard clapt (dialect word meaning stuck) *close under his chin, with a blue place on ye small of his back, his face all blood, with a wooden tabacca-box and three short tabacca pipes in his pocket all unbroken. She then forthwith called unto certain of her neighbours who helped to carry this her father home, where he was kept till he was carried upon Tuesday following unto ye church and there buried. This she further sayeth that she found her fathers belt tyed on a Knot to ye buckle a great way above ye place where she had formaly found her father lying dead.'*

Stickle Tarn

Edward Benson of High-close, another witness, at his Examination, after being duely sworn and refered to as the examinate *'sayeth that he being ye 30th day of June last past at Langdale Mill in ye said county, one William Harrison of ye Ellers in Langdale aforesaid came then and there upon him, and as hee and this examinate were going thence towards their respected homes in a place called ye Becks this examinate said unto the said William Harrison - 'it is strange that William Dixon of Millfell-place (who was as this examinate hath heard found dead upon Langdale-fell at a place called sloat-foot upon ye 14th of April last past early in the morning by Catherine Dixon his daughter, and was seen by this examinate lying dead upon his bed late that evening) should come so upon his death having no more wound upon him than he had, to which William Harrison replied we kill'd him. Then this examinate replied, 'was there never a spark of Grace in thy heart, nor thy father's nor thy mother's nor in none of all you three', to which the said William Harrison answered and said, 'we had ill luck to do that ill deed unto him', meaning as this examinate verily believeth, ye said William Dixon. And ye said William Harrison did then desire this examinate that he would not take part with ye daughter of the said William Dixon, saying that if this examinate did so, he were then but dead.'*

Edward Benson must have been shocked by this statement.

Another shorter examination has survived, that of Jo: Johnston of Johnston Place in Langdale;

'He deposeth and sayeth that he heard Robert Harrison of Robinson-place in Langdale when he was carring William Dixon of Milfell-place upon a Biear to be buried at ye Church say that the said Will. Dixon did bleed upon him.'

Note: It was a belief at that time, that a murdered corpse would bleed when touched by the murderer.

An unusual statement was taken from *'Robert Tunstall of .... house in Selside in ye County of Westmorland yeoman upon this oath said that he believes one Robert Harrison of Landdale, waller, did strike with a Rule one Will Dixon late of Langdale upon the head ye 14th day of April last past a little before day, on which wound he believes he dyed. And he Knows this to be true by his Art in Geomancy'*, (which my dictionary describes as 'divination by figures of or on earth'.)

Isabell Dixon of Millbeck in Langdale, spinster was bound in £20 to *'prosente and preferr a Bill of Judition at ye next Assises to be holden at Appleby against Robert Harrison and William Harrison of Ellers in Langdale.'* Edward Benson was also bound in the same sum to give evidence against the Harrisons. Catherine Dixon and Jo: Johnston were both bound in the sum of £10 to appear.
Not only was Jo: Johnston bound to give evidence he was also *'bound together with Ro: Satterthwaite of ye Longhouse in £40 apiece to make sure that Ro. & Will. Harrison appeared at the assizes.'*

Interesting what you come across when simply tracing the history of your family! I have both Dixon and Harrison ancestors, but do not know if either of these are related.

More Hirds and some Tysons

John Hird, born 1717, the eldest son of William[1] and Elizabeth of 'The Oaks', appears eventually to have gone to live at Langdale; he had two sons and four daughters. His elder son, John, married Mary Robinson, his second son James, born in 1767, is thought to have married twice and also to have had a son James, born in 1801, who died in infancy and then another James, born in 1809.

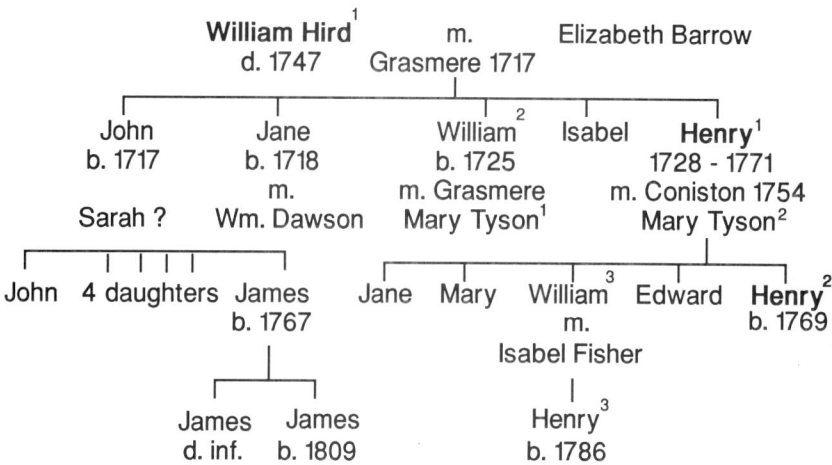

William and Elizabeth's second son, William[2], born in 1725, married a Mary Tyson[1] at Grasmere in 1752 and, to make matters more confusing, their youngest son, Henry Hird[1], my ancestor, also married a Mary Tyson[2] in 1754 at Coniston. This Mary was born at Eskdale 1729 the eldest child of Edward Tyson and Dorothy Nicholson of Bridge End. Mary[2] had five younger sisters, and her parents eventually moved to Hall Garth, Tilberthwaite, after which her only brother, Edward, was born in 1745. (see p. 123)

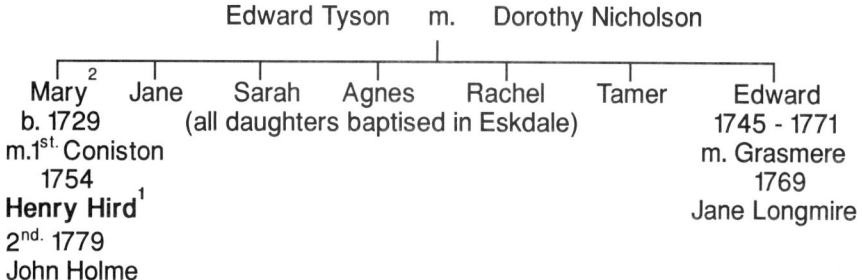

High Hall Garth

It has taken only a few minutes to type these last few lines, but it took me at least ten years to find Mary Tyson[2]'s baptism! There had been Tysons at Tilberthwaite from early years, so I researched all the parishes around - to no avail. It was not until I re-read her father's will that I got the clue; he refered to his brother-in-law Thomas Hartley of Church House, Eskdale. By this time I knew who Thomas's wife was, but that line will be dealt with in another chapter. I still do not know the reason for the family moving to Tilberthwaite.

Mary[2]'s brother, Edward Tyson, married Jane Longmire of Grasmere, by Licence, on November 10th. 1769; sadly, she died in March 1770 and Edward died the following year, without issue. Mary, being the eldest sister inherited Hall Garth. Edward, in his will, made Henry Hird[1], his brother-in-law, his executor. Probate was granted on July 1st. 1771. On the 4th. August, just five weeks later, Henry[1] made his will which was proved by his executors, John Hird, his brother, Christopher Roberts, his cousin, John Brockbank of Birdhow, his neighbour and friend and George Mackereth, his cousin, just twelve days later on August 16th.

Poor Mary, in a short time she had lost both brother and husband and was left with five children, the eldest thirteen and the youngest three. Henry[1] had left instructions for his estates to be sold to provide for her and the children and sixteen shillings yearly towards the maintenance of Elizabeth, his mother (née Barrow).

Henry's executors could not have had an easy task either; as well as his estate to sort, he left them with his brother-in-law's as well. Mary, as Edward Tyson's heir, became Customary Tenant of Hall Garth, but I have not been able to find the Admittance. She was, however, living there in 1779 when she married John Holme and continued to do so.

Low Hall Garth

Little is known of the childhood of Mary's children, but she must have been able to support them.

William[3], the eldest son of Henry[1] and Mary[2], on the 30[th.] May 1786, married Isabel Fisher and on 21[st.] December the same year, baptised his son Henry. The marriage entry describes William as a slate-getter of the parish of Ulverston.

Ancient parish boundaries can be very confusing to researchers not familiar with them. Even though Tilberthwaite was miles away from Ulverston, it was part of its large parish, just as Eskdale was within the parish of St. Bees and Birker in the parish of Millom.

William[3] eventually went to live at Kelletground in the parish of Kirkby Ireleth and here, on 14[th.] of September 1798, he received notice that he had been chosen by lot to serve in the Supplementary Militia, a copy of this survives, and appeared in the August 1978 News Letter of the Cumbria F.H.S. It is not known if he served or provided a substitute, as was allowed.

On 13th. March 1800, with son Henry[3], he signed the Apprentice Indenture for the said son Henry to be

'. . . taught, informed and instructed, or caused and procured to be taught, informed and instructed, by William Bellman of Broughton-in-Furness, in the Art and Mystery of Clock and Watch-making for a term of six and a half years.' (Indenture CRO Barrow)

Young Henry[3] was a few months short of his fourteenth birthday. In the same year, Isabel, his mother, died at the age of thirtyfour.

Henry[2], my great, great grandfather, was sent to Ulpha, to serve an apprenticeship at the Crook to become a blacksmith. I have spent many hours searching for (and not finding) his Indenture, nor do I know who was his master, but I suspect it was Henry Tyson a kinsman of his mother's. So I have to quote tradition. When, as a small child, I asked my uncle, 'Where did the Hirds come from?' he replied 'From Langdale, the first Henry came to serve his time as a blacksmith, paying two shillings and sixpence per week for the use of the tools. Each Saturday afternoon he went to visit his mother and returned on Sunday night. When his master died he was left the smithy'. There is always some truth in tradition.

Once he was well established as a blacksmith at the Crook, Ulpha, Henry's thoughts turned to matrimony. Instead of walking home to Tilberthwaite, he went in the other direction, to Birker, to do his courting. On January 2nd. 1803, he married Mary Bateman of Penny Hill at Eskdale Church. She was the daughter of Henry Bateman and Hannah Nicholson.

Penny Hill

The Batemans

There were Batemans in the area from early times, but I could not place this Henry with any of them and it was not until I saw the Enfranchisement papers of Penny Hill that I stumbled on the clue.

In the 18c many yeomen were enfranchising their tenements and Henry and Hannah were no exception. What did it entail? 'Money'! They were the Customary Tenants of Penny Hill, Spot How and Piet Nest, so, to complete the deal they had to borrow money. The tenements were actually the property of Hannah, refered to as *'Hannah Nicholson now the wife of Henry Bateman'*.

> *For an Ancient Messuage and Tenement called Spothow*
> *For an Ancient Messuage and Tenement called Penny Hill*
> (a separate sheet for Piet Nest)

Viz.	*Thirtyfive Years Purchase of the Customary*	£ 40. 2. 1
	Rents of the said Tenements being together	£ 1. 2.11

> *Seventeen years and an half purchase of the*
> *Town Term Rent of No. 21 (Penney Hill)*
> *being 3s/4d*   £   2.18.11
> *No. 20 (Spot How) pays no Town Term*

> *Five Fines computing the same at Twenty*
> *Times The Ancient Yearly Customary Rent*
> *each Tenement*   £114.11. 8

There was money for Heriots, for Boon Services, two Bracken Boons, for Mill Service, for the service of Two Carriages and for Wood now growing on the Tenements. A similar list for Piet Nest, which resulted in Hannah and Henry borrowing (in 1779) £400 from Stephen Nicholson of Randlehow at 4%. The heading of the document is as follows:

'*Know all Men by these presents That we Henry Bateman and Hannah his Wife and Elizabeth Nicholson, Widow* (Hannah's mother) *of Penny Hill in Birker in the parish of Millom and County of Cumberland and John Bateman of Colleth in the Parish of Grasmere and County of Westmorland*' etc.

Had I not seen the above document, with its reference to John Bateman of Colwith, I might never have found Henry Bateman's roots. This enabled me to go back another two generations, but I am still at a loss to establish whether the Batemans are a Cumberland or Westmorland family.

An Indenture dated Eighth day of June 1682 (D/Pen/27 CRO) between Sir William Pennington of Muncaster, Bart. and Henry Bateman, now of Colleth:

'*For and in consideration of Twentyfour Pounds of Lawful money of England to him in his hand given by Henry Bateman now of Colleth released to the said Henry One Messuage or Tenement situated, lying and being at Colleth in Little Langdale in the county of Westmorland*'

The first Bateman entry in the register is 1[st.] April 1682 when Margaret, daughter of Henry Bateman, was baptised. From Henry's will and the registers I have been able to compile a tree

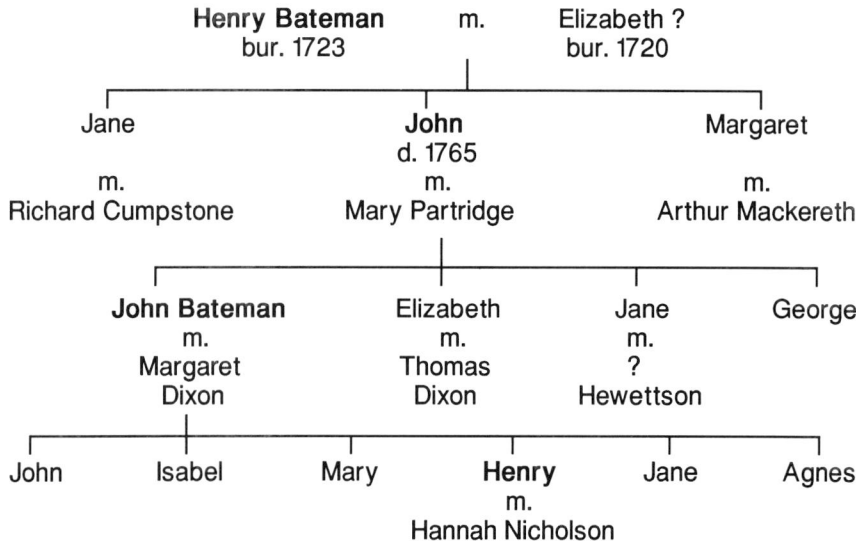

I am extremely grateful to Mr. E.R. Lewtas Gregson of Kirkcaldy, Fife who very kindly extracted for me, from the the deeds of both tenements at Colwith, all the interesting items.

There are two endorsements on the deeds, one of which is a faint note on the outside:

'Enfranchise Deed from Sr. Wm. Pennington of the low estate at Colloth':

'memo. That this tenth day of June Ano Dni. 1682 Nicholas Ecclestone the within named attorney did enter into one messuage called Colloth and one cloase ... and did deliver quiet and peaceable possession and seisin unto the within named Henry Bateman in his proper person.... by delivery of the latch of his said house door, and a clod of Earthe and a twigge of wood together with this present deed'.

The witnesses were:- Anthony Knipe, John Bowman, William Dixon, Leonard Benson, and Will. Sawrey (who seemed to sign most documents or wills). Nicholas Ecclestone was most likely the lawyer.

Henry Bateman died in January 1723 and, from his inventory, it appears he had retired from farming as it consisted of Purse and apparel, money owing to him and bonds to the value of £49.3s.; one of the apprizers was Will. Sawrey.

In 1712, John Bateman, his son, bought two thirds of a close or pasture called Wilson Hackett, from John Wilson, of Truss Gapp in Swinndale, farmer and Anthony Wilson, now of High Wray in Claife, rough mason, for £10.

In 1728, on September 30th, Edward Rigg of Collwith, miller, sells *'all his lands, messuages, tenements, etc., together with his water grist or corn mill which he Edward purchased of Richard Cumpstone, commonly known as Collwith Mill, with two kilns and all materials & utensils thereto belonging, together with 3 peat mosses which he purchased else where; the whole being conveyed to his son William Rigg, for the sum of £120.'*

In 1750, William Rigg of Hawkshead, slate dealer, mortgages the Mill to George Holme of Walthwaite, yeoman, for three years. Amount advanced - £120. William Rigg was unable to discharge his mortgage as, in 1756 *'Nov. 16th. Wm. Rigg of Roger Ground in the Bayliffwick of Hawkshead Slatemerchant and George Holme of Walthwaythe'* sold the Mill to John Bateman of Keen Ground, Hawkshead, yeoman, for £285.2s.

John Bateman died in October 1765 describing himself as *'of Colwith in Little Langdale, yeoman'* His will, made 8th October 1765 and proved eight days later, devises: *'to his son and heir John Bateman (younger) All his lands etc. at Colwith or elsewhere in Little Langdale: yearly free rent 3d. Also the Close called Smith Hackett a parcel of the inheritance of Sir John Pennington of Muncaster and of the ancient yearly rent of 1s 7d.; to hold 'according to the customs of Little Langdale'* on condition that his son John *'allow Mary my Wife the High Dwelling House and fire fuel for one fire during her life, and also pay to her an anuity of £8,'* and also the following legacies; *'£20 to my daughter Jane Hewettson, widow, at Candlemas come a year after my decease, £40 to John Dixon my grandson son of Thomas Dixon when he shall attain the age of 21 years if then living; also £140 to George Bateman my second son to be paid by my Executrix out of my personal estate at Candlemas come a year after my decease.'*

He makes his wife, Mary, executrix and residuary legatee, but nominated John Brockbank of Birdhow and Roger Wood of Brow, both in Little Langdale to see that everything is carried out as he has appointed and leaves them ten shillings apiece for their trouble.

In 1769, Mary Bateman, now of Foxhouses near Whitehaven in the parish of St. Bees, Cumberland, widow, relinquishes all right and claim to the Colwith property in return for an extra guinea per year in addition to her already existing £8 paid by her son John Bateman. What was Mary doing in St. Bees?

In November 1770, John Bateman bought the close Smith Hackett from Sir Joseph Pennington and also enfranchised the two tenements at Colwith, somewhat cheaper than the Birker properties, just £24.16.8d. By 1782, John Bateman was evidently in difficulties and mortgaged the farm to Arthur Mackereth for £500 the only burden on the title being his mother's £8 plus one guinea. Did the money borrowed by his brother have an effect on John? After legal battles he finally left the property in 1789. The Bateman Family had been there just over a hundred years. Apart from my direct line I have nothing on the other Westmorland Batemans.

It is interesting to note future events. Between 1793 and 1796 the two Colwith properties were sold to the curate of Langdale and several vicars or curates of Cartmel Fell, Crosthwaite and Ings or Hugill, representing *'The Governors of the Bounty of Queen Anne'* the income from them to help the Poor Clergy. I believe one of the later tenants was Lanty Slee renowned for his illegal whisky!

Was the Margaret Dixon who married John Bateman or Thomas Dixon who married Elizabeth Bateman connected with the murder? With all families it is difficult to follow all the lines, but it's a funny old game family history, how, when you are looking for something quite different you find a missing link.

Colwith

More Hirds

When considering the children of Henry Hird[1] and his wife, Mary Tyson[2], I have mentioned William and Henry but have not accounted for Jane, Mary and Edward.

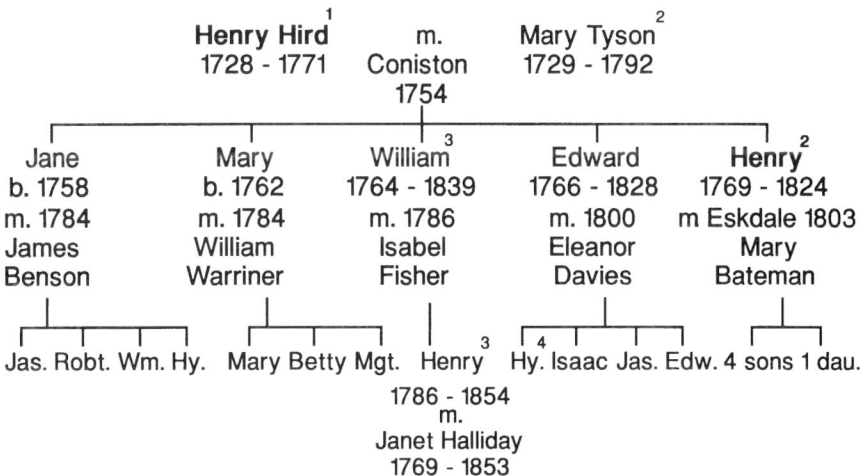

Henry Hird[1]   m.   Mary Tyson[2]
1728 - 1771   Coniston   1729 - 1792
1754

Jane	Mary	William[3]	Edward	**Henry**[2]
b. 1758	b. 1762	1764 - 1839	1766 - 1828	1769 - 1824
m. 1784	m. 1784	m. 1786	m. 1800	m Eskdale 1803
James	William	Isabel	Eleanor	Mary
Benson	Warriner	Fisher	Davies	Bateman

Jas. Robt. Wm. Hy.   Mary Betty Mgt.   Henry[3]   Hy.[4] Isaac Jas. Edw.   4 sons 1 dau.

Henry[3]
1786 - 1854
m.
Janet Halliday
1769 - 1853

Mary married William Warriner at Ambleside in 1784; Edward[1] married Eleanor Davies in 1800 and Jane married James Benson at Colton in 1784, he was a blacksmith, living and working at Busk in Ambleside. His descendants continued as blacksmiths, in the same place, until 1999. The illustration shows the smithy and a device used for tyring cart wheels.

Edward Hird[1] is described in the registers as a weaver, however, from family letters that have survived, it appears that Edward also had some land and that both Bensons and Hirds lived at Busk.

Of their early years nothing is known; in 1828, Edward Hird[1] died and Henry[4] was his heir at Law, however, I think Edward's wife, Eleanor, had an interest in the estate.

According to Parson & Whites 1829 Directory, Henry Hird[4], boot and shoe maker and a James Benson (whether father or son I do not know) were living *'below Stockgill'* and Isaac Hird, bobbin manufacturer, was living at Gill Close, above Stockgill. In 1830, Henry was negotiating to buy property in Coniston and arrange a mortgage on his own. He obviously got the property as his brother Isaac was conducting his bobbin manufacturing there when he took on Ambleside parish poor boys as apprentices.

By 1833, solicitors were pressing both Henry[4] and his mother, Eleanor for money and Henry was writing to Uncle William, now living in Eskdale, with all kinds of schemes to make money. Uncle William was also writing letters to his son, Henry[3], watch and clock maker in Dumfries, urging him to make a will as he had no family, and telling him in no uncertain terms that Henry[4] of Ambleside would claim the lot if he didn't.

Later in 1833, Henry[4] was in gaol awaiting trial at the next assizes (Quarter sessions Appleby Mar. 1834). *'charged with aiding and abetting one Robert Benson at Ambleside by firing a loaded gun & wounding Isaac Wilson'* (from a list of prisoners under confinement in the County Gaol and House of Correction at Appleby, at Michaelmas Quarter Sessions, 18th. October 1833.) His board from January 3rd. to March 7th. 1834, at 4d per day came to £1.1s. Robert Benson was not held at the same gaol. The outcome of the trial is not known.

I think perhaps the letter from a solicitor to Uncle William[3] sums up the two families.

'Ambleside 1837. Robert Benson is leading the life of a Drunkard and Blackguard. I lent him £35 to enable him to commence Business to which he pays no attention. The Iron & Tools are all rusted in the shop. I am determined to have my money repaid immediately or sell all of which he is possessed. His Brothers Henry & William are addicted to drinking but I see nothing but honest intentions. Your sister (Jane Hird) *had a troublesome life the short time she survived her husband. I think your Relation Henry Hird of Busk is Not possessed of good Principles, at least I form no good Opinion of him. The two Children of the late James Benson jun. Are both fine Children and I find that I shall have as much overplus as will support them responsibly During minority and a handsom fortune when they attain 21 years.'*

Henry and Eleanor's property was sold in 1837 and the movement of these families after Uncle William died in 1839 is obscure, until cousin Henry[3] of Dumfries died - but more of that later.

TO BE SOLD,

BY AUCTION,

At the Salutation Hotel,

AMBLESIDE,

At Six o'Clock on Wednesday Evening, the 4th Day of January, 1837,

(BY ORDER OF THE MORTGAGEE)

Three Dwelling

HOUSES,

WITH A

Good Orchard, Garden, &c.

Situate at *Busk*, in Ambleside, in the occupation of Mrs. ELEANOR HIRD and others.

Mr. POOLE, of *Gill Head*, Bowness, will afford further Information.

Gill Head, 30th December, 1836.

Stephen Soulby, Printer, Market-place, Ulverston.

More Social History

It may surprise readers that, during the 1820's, and 30's, there was much poverty in the area. Between June 1826 and 1827, in Ambleside, no fewer than 160 persons received parish relief, some in money others in clothing or rent. In 1832 the Matron of the workhouse was allowed £2 in the year, payable weekly, to find tea and sugar and an extra 6d a week for butter. £5 per year was allowed to find clothes for herself and her two daughters. The inmates fared much worse.

Workhouse Diet

Breakfast & Supper	*Porridge & Milk*
Dinner Monday	*Offal & Potatoes*
Dinner Tuesday	*Offal & Potatoes*
Dinner Wednesday	*Boiled Rice*
Dinner Thursday (Banquet?)	*Herrings, Bacon & Potatoes*
Dinner Friday	*Offal & Potatoes*
Dinner Saturday	*Offal & Potatoes*
Dinner Sunday	*Boiled Rice*

Ref. Ambleside Vestry Accounts

Parish children were apprenticed as soon as possible. As I said earlier, both Henry and Isaac Hird took some. Children were also sent to the cotton mills. The terms I quote from a letter to the Overseer:

'As soon as the children begin to attend we allow each 2d a day, merely by way of encouragment as they cannot even earn that until they have learnt. As they become more useful their wages are increased according to the work done by each person. In the course of 9 to 12 months they will probably earn from 4 to 5 shillings.

*We are **not allowed to take children under 9 years old**. Our hours of attendence are from six in the morning until half-past seven at night, allowing half an hour for breakfast and an hour for dinner.'*

Appalling conditions, yet these children survived and many of their descendants today hold high places in society.

Another letter which has survived is from Henry Hird[3] of Dumfries, written in March 1836, which is interesting from a Social History point of view;

'.... have had boisterous winter hear (sic) *of wind and heavy rain. On 23.rd January was an uncommon day of Black weather almost ever witnessed by the oldest inhabitants in the country. I left our place on the Monday after for Kilmarnock and Glasgow and it is not uncommonn to see the plantation of trees torn up by their roots, there was a planting of fir wood about six miles from Kilmarnock that one would have said every third tree was blown down .....'*

He remarks about houses being destroyed by the gale in Glasgow and while he was there, of thunder, wind and large hailstones. He mentions Edward, his cousin, (from Moorhouse) and then a bit more Social History;

'We have a number of families going away to America this Season selling all of to sail in April to New York.
    Our markets rather higher than they have been this some time back. A good deal of trouble has been here and a number of uncomon Sudden Deaths. Just dropped down dead.
    I shall be in the south as soon as the weather will permit but will sail straight from Dumfries and to it again.'

It was the practice of the Overseers of the poor to give their parish paupers a chance to go overseas and Ambleside was no exception in this. From the same source as before mentioned, in 1832, William Clark and his family were allowed £30 and were to sail on the 21[st.] of April of that year from Maryport, on the Brig *Nicholson*. As this ship was to carry upwards of fifty emigrants it was compelled to have on board a surgeon. The shipping agent in Whitehaven, arranging this exodus, thought the duty levied by Colonial Law might not operate on these emigrants, if so it would be the means of sending them to Upper Canada free. There were eight in the Clark family and the recommended list of provisions was:

1½ cwt Hard Bread, say, Sea Biscuits	*at 21/- per cwt*
2 cwt Bacon, Ham & Hung Beef	*at 6/- per stone*
1½ cwt Oatmeal	*at 2/- per stone*
3 or 4 stones of Flour	*at 2/6 per stone*
16 to 20 stones of potatoes	*at 2d per stone*

It was suggested that Twenty shillings be spent on Groceries:- molasses, butter etc.

The bedding allowed was:-

7/6 for two Straw mattresses
7/- a piece for six blankets
7/6 a piece for two rugs

They must have slept four to a mattress, but, like thousands more, the Clarks sailed away to a new life.

Maryport Pier
(from *'Ports and Harbours of Great Britain'*
date and publisher unknown)

Moorhouse

Hirds in Ulpha, at Moorhouse

Our story now takes us back to Cumberland, to my own ancestors Henry Hird[2] and Mary Bateman. In 1818 they restored one of the cottages of the hamlet that was known as the Crook, and called it Moorhouse, it is close to the smithy. If you compare this house with the Oaks at Loughrigg you will see that it is built on similar lines. Here they produced their family. The first child, Henry, died as a baby.

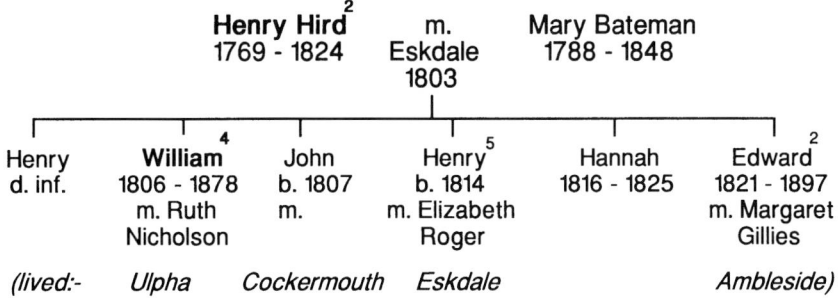

		Henry Hird[2] 1769 - 1824	m. Eskdale 1803	Mary Bateman 1788 - 1848	
Henry d. inf.	**William**[4] 1806 - 1878 m. Ruth Nicholson	John b. 1807 m.	Henry[5] b. 1814 m. Elizabeth Roger	Hannah 1816 - 1825	Edward[2] 1821 - 1897 m. Margaret Gillies
(lived:-	*Ulpha*	*Cockermouth*	*Eskdale*		*Ambleside)*

They were an enterprising couple; blacksmiths in those days were very busy people, there would be a great deal of activity at the smithy, mending farm implements, shoeing horses and making parts for anything that was metal, including clocks. But even so Henry was also a businessman. In 1802, together with John Dawson of Seathwaite, yeoman, Robert Jackson of Broughton-in-Furness, hooper, and William Dawson of Ulpha, slate-getter, they took from the Lord of the Manor a Lease of land and *'All that Slate Quarry situated in the Manor of Ulpha'.* He also held a mortgage on Robert Jenkinson's property at Biggartmire; Mary kept the village shop.

The Smithy at Moorhouse

On November 25[th.] 1824, tragedy struck, Henry[2] died. I was told that his death was caused by falling between the horse and cart shafts while delivering groceries; it could be true, as he made his will on the 24th *'being sickly in body and considering the uncertainty of human life'.* He was buried on the 27[th.], aged 55 years.

He left estate to the value of £1,500, the interest of half to be paid to his wife Mary, and she he appointed Executrix. The trustees were William[3] his brother, William Bateman his brother-in-law and William Hird[4] his eldest son.

:

By the time of his death, Henry[2] and his family had accumulated more land. Henry had bought the Nook when Mrs Hannah Allason proposed its sale by public auction; he bought it for £414. In 1823, at the age of 17 years, his son William had bought Esphole for £200.

At the time of his father's death, William[4] was eighteen and he carried on the business of blacksmith, whilst his mother continued to keep the shop.

Little is known of the family for the next twenty years, as no letters have survived. Mary Hird (Bateman) of Moorhouse became the eldest family member after the death of her brother-in-law William Hird[3], (born in 1764 at the Oaks, Loughrigg), died at Hollinhow in Eskdale in 1839 and was buried there. However, tragedy struck again in February 1848 and the sad events are well documented.

Elias Casson, a young man in the valley, kept a diary and in the entry for February 4[th.] 1848, he reported misty conditions. Mary Hird was due to go over to Eskdale on that day, to attend the funeral of Sarah Porter and to visit her son and grandchildren and her brother. She was to have been picked up by a gig, but somehow missed it and set off walking over Birker Moor, making for her brother's house at Penny Hill; the mist thickened and Mary was lost. When she didn't arrive, no one worried - they just thought she had changed her mind. It was several days later, when a neighbour who had attended the funeral, called at Moorhouse to ask the reason for her absence, that it was realised that she was missing. She was found on 10[th.] of February and buried at Ulpha two days later.

Mary Hird had been a well respected member of the community and has been mentioned in several books. I quote from *'The Old Man'* by A.C. Gibson, published in 1849, a year after her death. He refers to her as *'A Noble Peasant'* who with hand *'open as day to melting Charity'* possesses a heart ready to acknowledge and to sympathise with goodness whether it appears in the disposition and the works of peasant, parson, peer or prince. He continues:

'She was by no means a common character. Left a widow many years ago with a young family, by great industry and exertion she brought them up and settled them in the world in useful and respectable callings' He then describes where in the Duddon Dale --- *Stands a neat and roomy cottage and a garden, well furnished with bee-hives and flowers. Here she kept a small shop for the sale of groceries and draper's ware. With a manner and outside somewhat plain and countrified, she had as kind a heart as ever beat in the human bosom. She appeared almost to keep open house, and gave away, I should think,*

more bread and cheese and home brewed, than is sold in some public houses. If you called at haytime at the well whitewashed house, the fireplace, and all was beautiful to behold; and in the large grate was an immense thick sod of purple heather in full bloom, the prettiest chimney ornament I ever saw.

I have occasionlly boarded in the cottage for a week at a time, and never saw anyone applying for relief go away empty-handed. Few indeed, in a contracted sphere, have been so generally respected; and long will it be e'er that pleasant valley loses an inhabitant so beloved and respected by rich and poor as Mary Hird'.

William Hird[4], Mary's son, continued at Moorhouse as a blacksmith. Sadly, his wife, Ruth (Nicholson) died, just a month after his mother, leaving him with six children, the youngest, Edward[3], a small baby.

The Census Return for Moorhouse in 1851 reads as follows:

William Hird[4]	H widower	45	Blacksmith with 4 acres	b.	Ulpha
John	" S	12	Blacksmith apprentice	b.	"
Hannah	" D	10	Scholar	b.	"
Jane	" D	7	Scholar	b.	"
Edward[3]	" S	3		b.	"
Esther Nicholson	U	23	House servant	b.	Gos-forth
William Dawson	H M	43	Slate merchant & Grocer	b.	Sea-thwaite
Sarah "	W M	42			"
Mary A. Harrington, nie		11	Educated at home	b.	Irton
Jane Dawson Sis	U	26	Cook seeking situation	b.	Ulpha

Notes: 1) Esther Nicholson, shown as a servant, was a relative.
2) Moorhouse had been divided into two separate dwellings, the grocery business having been taken over by another relative, W. Dawson.
3) The John Hird (aged 12), was the Author's grandfather.
4) Two of William's sons, Henry[6] and William[5] had already left home and were apprenticed.

It is interesting to note that the seventh generation of descendents from Henry[2] and Mary are now being brought up at Moorhouse.

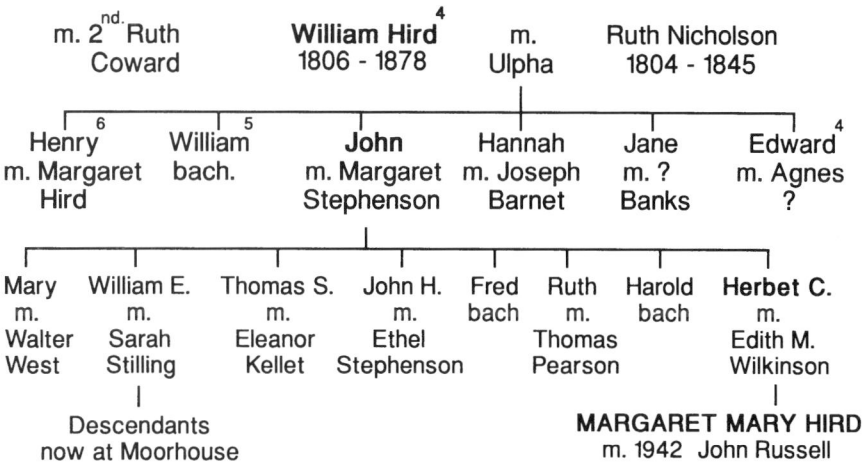

m. 2nd. Ruth **William Hird**[4] m. Ruth Nicholson
Coward 1806 - 1878 Ulpha 1804 - 1845

Henry[6] William[5] **John** Hannah Jane Edward[4]
m. Margaret bach. m. Margaret m. Joseph m. ? m. Agnes
Hird Stephenson Barnet Banks ?

Mary William E. Thomas S. John H. Fred Ruth Harold **Herbet C.**
m. m. m. m. bach m. bach m.
Walter Sarah Eleanor Ethel Thomas Edith M.
West Stilling Kellet Stephenson Pearson Wilkinson

Descendants **MARGARET MARY HIRD**
now at Moorhouse m. 1942 John Russell

Ping-pong at Moorhouse in 1903

Hirds who left Ulpha.

Of the children of Henry Hird[2] and Mary Bateman, only the eldest, William[4] remained in the Duddon Valley. John, sixteen when his father died, was apprenticed to an ironmonger in Ulverston; after finishing his apprenticship, he went to London where he married. Eventually he settled in Cockermouth, where, in September 1841, when Henry Dixon, of Market Place, Cockermouth, retired, John took over the *'Grocery and Ironmongery Business'*. In the local press he advertised his wares, I quote;

'The Recent reductions in the Prices of Tea and Sugar enables JH to offer them on reduced Terms. Families will find a very useful Tea at 5s per lb: inferior ditto lower: good strong Congou (black tea) *5s.6d: very fine ditto 6s: very fine Young Hyson* (green tea) *6s: very superior Gunpowder* (top quality green tea) *8s per lb: finest roasted Coffee 2s 2d per lb: inferior ditto lower, with every other Article on the most reasonable Terms.'*

He listed amongst the ironmongery:- cutlery, a variety of articles in Britannia Metal and Berlin Silver. He catered for farmers and for builders.

John had a family of six, five girls and one son, who in 1879 cut his throat. According to the inquest, he was a crack shot at the range where he was a member.
Elizabeth, one of his daughters, married Ferdinando James and produced into the teens of children. Later, John was to take his son-in-law into partnership.
The late Dr. Boyes of Gosforth has produced a James family tree of which there is a copy in the Carlisle Record Office.

The third son, Henry[5], ten when his father died, became a blacksmith and grocer at Eskdale where he married Elizabeth Rogers and produced four sons and two daughters. Two of his grandsons, John and Joseph Hird, were killed in the First World War. Joseph won the Military Medal, which is now in the possession of *his* grandsons who live in Bury St. Edmunds, keeping the 'Hird' name going.

Hannah, Henry[2] and Mary's only daughter, died shortly after her father.

Edward[3], their youngest son, went to Dumfries, to his cousin, Henry Hird[3], to learn *'the art of Clock and watch making.'*

Hird clockmakers

When Henry Hird[3], son of William[3] became apprenticed to Bellman of Broughton in 1800, he started a line

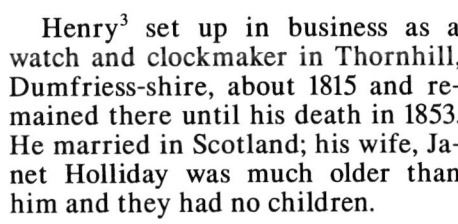

of Hird clock and watchmakers, no fewer than seven of whom are listed in Loomes *'Watchmakers and Clockmakers of the World'*

Henry[3] set up in business as a watch and clockmaker in Thornhill, Dumfriess-shire, about 1815 and remained there until his death in 1853. He married in Scotland; his wife, Janet Holliday was much older than him and they had no children.

After the death of his uncle, Henry[2], he took his young cousin, Edward[3] as an apprentice. Edward worked well, and when he left Thornhill, moved to Edinburgh where he continued his training with Bryson in Princes Street. Edward, too, married a Scots girl, Margaret Gillies and they moved to England, where he set up a business in Ambleside. In due course, Edward[3] trained three of his nephews, Henry[6], William[5] and Edward[4], the sons of William[4] and his own two sons, Henry[7] and William[6]. In their turn, some of these passed on their skills to the next generation, Edward's grandson, Henry[8], and a son and grandson of John Hird of Moorhouse, (b. 1839).

Thus, various branches of the family set up business in Ulverston and Barrow, as well as continuing the Ambleside shop until the early years of the Second World War.

At least three long-case clocks survive in the family, two by Henry[3] of Thornhill and one by Edward[3] of Ambleside.

Hirds back in Westmorland

Edward Hird[3] and Margaret Gillies had six children, but only three survived to adulthood. Their daughter, Margaret, (b. 1847) married R.P. Hunter and lived in Ambleside, at 'The Nook' until her death in 1924. She had seven children, three sons and four daughters. The Hunters celebrated their Golden Wedding in 1922, the celebrations were recorded in the Westmorland Gazette.

Both their sons, Henry[7] and William[6] became watch and clock makers. Henry married Emma Scaife, a school teacher in Ambleside. But from their three children, only one grandchild was produced.

William married Elizabeth Stalker of Ambleside and it was she who continued the Ambleside shop for many years after her husband's death. William and Elizabeth had two sons and five daughters. Neither son married so the name died out. One daughter married and went to live in Vancouver; we are in touch with her descendants. A second married and has descendants in Yorkshire. These two are the only ones of the family with descendants. Muriel, another of William's daughters, was, in her early days, teaching in Russia when the Revolution started and later for many years taught at Ackworth School in Yorkshire. She ended her days at Ambleside leaving her books to the Armitt Library.

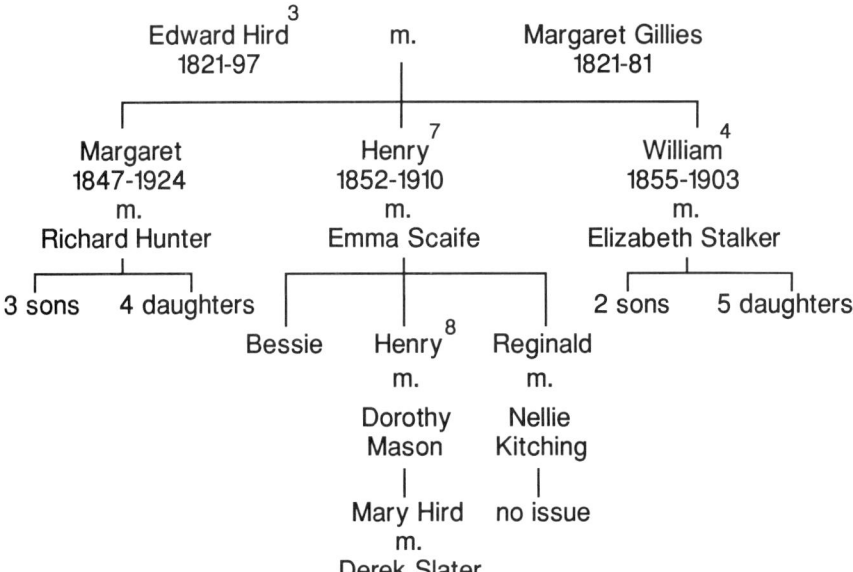

Death of Henry Hird of Thornhill.

Little is known about the Hird cousins from 1840 until the following announcement appeared in the Whitehaven paper the *Cumberland Pacquet* in the issue of August 29[th.] 1854.

'On Sunday last, awfully sudden, at the house of Mr. Wm Kennaugh, Quay Street, in this town, where he had been on a visit for a few days, **Mr Henry Hird** [(3)], *watchmaker, Thornhill, Scotland, and formerly of Eskdale, in this county, much and deservedly respected'.*

There is a saying "Where there is a Will there are relatives". There is another one which adds "where there isn't one there are more". The Hirds were no exception, Henry had not left a will. He had thirteen surviving cousins who all put in a claim, as did his late wife's family.

Tree to show Henry of Thornhill and his cousins.

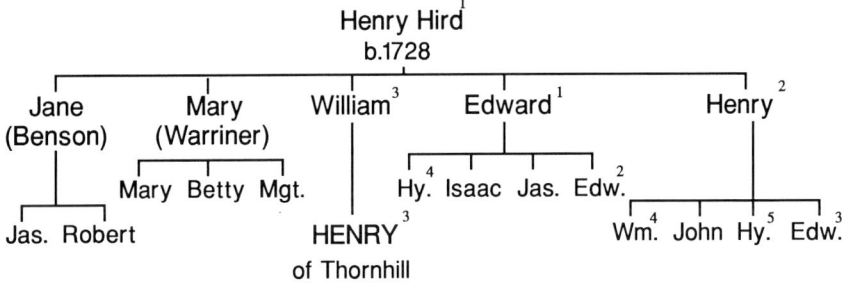

But first, because Henry had died suddenly, there was an inquest. An account of it appears in the same issue of the *Pacquet*. It must have somewhat shocked some of his cousins, but maybe not all! I quote:

'From the evidence of a young man named James Scott, it appears that he met the deceased about nine o'clock in Queen St., and was requested by him to show him the way to the Post Office in Roper Street. Scott did so and afterwards at the deceased's request, took him to Mrs Cowan's eating house where he was staying. The old man (he was 65!) was then tipsy, but not so much so as to be unable to walk and know what he was about.

Mrs Cowan, the proprietress of the eating house, deposed, that The deceased was by trade a watchmaker, and had been in the habit of stopping at her house on his visits to Whitehaven from his residence in Thornhill in Dumfries, for the last twenty-two years.

Since the death of his wife, which occurred about nine months ago, he had taken very much to the habit of drinking. He arrived as usual on Thursday last, and then appeared in his customary health and spirits. on Sunday, he ate his dinner with some appetite and went out. In the evening he came back with the witness Scott, and still appeared well, and made no complaints. He ordered supper of cold roast beef and potatoes, of which he had just commenced to partake, when he was siezed with the symptoms of sickness, fell back in his chair and expired.

Dr. Wilson was sent for on the instant, and at once pronounced he was beyond all human aid. A police constable was called in and after removing the corpse upstairs, searched and took possession of the property found on the deceased, this consisted of two silver watches, a snuff box and other valuable securities to the amount of £1,352.11s. Of these an inventory was taken and the property handed over to the custody of the Suprintendant Clarke.'

The Coroner brought in a verdict of 'natural Death'. Mr. Brockbank, who had been solicitor to the deceased, was in attendance and stated that he had sent for the next of kin.

From The Cumberland Paquet on September 5th

'In our last we gave the remarkable sudden death of an aged man named Henry Hird while partaking his supper at an eating house in Quay Street. It will be remembered that upon the person deceased there was found money and valuables, the securities amounting to £1,352.16s and on subsequent examination of the property consisting of two carpet bags containing apparel in the one was found a small wooden box, carefully nailed down, which on being opened in the presence of two next of kin and Mr. Brockbank, was discovered one hundred and fifty-one sovereigns and seven old guineas. We find on enquiring that the deceased, as already stated was a watchmaker by trade, served his apprenticeship to Mr. Bellman of Broughton-in-Furness. He was not a scotchman by birth but a native of Eskdale in this county where several relatives survive him and where his remains were interred.'

Then the fun began! I think that the deceased must have been in contact with some of his cousins, those in Ulpha, Eskdale and Ambleside, although no correspondence has survived.

But for the surviving papers, especially the final Indenture of Settlement, I don't think I would have ever discovered the grandchildren of Henry Hird[1] and Mary Tyson.

The late Uncle William[3] had been right (Page 28) about Henry Hird[4], of Ambleside, (nicknamed 'Shoe Harry'), being the Heir at Law who was entitled to the Scottish property, but not the personal Estate.

Two firms of solicitors were dealing with the case, Armistead & Brockbank in Whitehaven and Studholm & Werr, Wigton. Christopher Harkness, Writer, of Dumfries was also involved. His full title would be 'Writer to the Signet', a member of an ancient society of solicitors in Scotland, who formerly had the exclusive right to prepare all summons and other writs pertaining to the Supreme Court of Justice and still have the exclusive privilege of preparing Crown writs.

From these lawyers' accounts, I have gained much information. At the time of the death, 'Shoe Harry' was reported as 'of Egremont', although I can find no trace of him there.

I quote from the account sent by Christopher Harkness to Messrs Edward Hird[3], watchmaker, Ambleside and William Hird[4], blacksmith, Ulpha, executors of the deceased Henry Hird, watchmaker, Thornhill.

'1854 Sept 21 To long consultation with you as to the succession of the late Henry Hird, Watchmaker, Thornhill to his heritable and moveable property - being doubtful whether it was regulated by the law of Scotland or England, also perusing Jn. McQueen's letter to you etc.'

The fee for this was thirteen shillings and four pence!

Oct 3. Letter from Messrs Armistead & Brockbank *'requesting me to do what was required to prevent Henry Hird* (Shoe Harry) *from being appointed Executor of the deceased.'*

By the 10th, another Writer, a Mr Smith of Thornhill was involved and by the 24th, Henry[4] had taken posession of the moveables at Thornhill and Mr Harkness was instructed to remove them, to prevent Henry dilapidating the Estate. Appraisers were engaged to value the goods, there were consultations between various solicitors and, by the 25th, it was decided that the sale of goods should take place immediately.

From the Studholme & Werr accounts:

'Nov 19th Having received a letter from Mr Smith of Dumfries, stating that he had lodged Henry Hird[(4)] in Gaol, on Nov 23rd they received from him a further letter saying that Henry was still in Prison and cautioning the Administrators not to demand or take anything

from Shankland on account of the balance due to the deceased, lest we should give Hy. Hird any grounds for an action for wrongful imprisonment.'

From surviving papers, we learn that Henry[4] had purchased goods at the sale and then refused to pay for them.

By the 24[th.], Isaac Hird ('Shoe Harry's brother) had put in an appearance.

I had lost track of him after he went to Coniston and, quite by chance, I was able to piece his movements together when I found him in the 1851 census at Low Mill in the parish of St John's Beckermet.
with his *wife, Ann b. Threlkeld,*
d. Ann b. Wes Thickham (?)
d. Mary and s. Edward, b. Keswick and
d. Lucy, b. Lancs. Sawrey

Among the papers is reference that he is late of Wigton, now of Virginia. He was a great 'wanderer', who was of the opinion that the late Mrs. Hird's relations were not entitled to anything from the Estate unless she had brought a dowry. The next weeks seem to be taken up with Isaac. There is one reference on Dec 3rd, which reads :-

'Attending Mr Edward Hird[(2)] *and conferring with him when he handed us a letter from his brother Isaac.'*

This throws another light on the family because, in the final settlement, Edward[2]'s address is New Hampshire in America, Isaac's as formerly of Crofton Hall nr Wigton, Cumberland, but now of America. They had come over for the settlement. Furthermore, in May 1856, a letter from 'Shoe Harry' to Studholme's enquired if his brother Isaac was still at Whins Mill and their findings that he was not.

Throughout, there has been reference to Henry[4], Edward[2] and Isaac Hird, but nothing other than *'James Hird, labourer'*. Is he the *'James Hird, blind pauper'* in the 1851 census, lodging in a house at Busk in Ambleside, next door to the Bensons?

Nothing is known of the Warriner sisters until the final settlement in 1857 when they were listed as follows :-
Mary Warriner, spinster, living in Preston, her sister Betty, wife of John Shaw, living in Manchester, and their sister Margaret, wife of Rev. John Graham of Sandbach in the county of Chester.

1856 April 2nd Studholme's received a letter from Isaac, requesting his brother's release from gaol and the final settlement was May 1857.

Accounts survive which were submitted by three sets of lawyers involved, they cover thirty three sides of closely written foolscap listing three hundred and one items. The total bill being £109.17.6

Henry[3]'s estate in England was £2990. 0. 3d., made up as follows, showing the capabilities of a businessman as well as those of a highly skilled clockmaker. (See photograph of clock on page 39)

	£	s.	d.
Cash in Whitehaven Joint Stock Bank	1003	3	6
Further cash in same bank	214	0	0
Mortgage on Casson property	600	0	0
Interest thereon to 14th Feb 1855			
less £1. 6. 2 property tax	31	3	10
Cash in the box found in deceased Carpet Bag	551	0	0
Debt due from William Watson £10 less 5s			
given to Commissioner of Police for his			
services in obtaining same Guineas in Carpet Bag	9	15	0
Seven one pound notes £7, Gold & Silver			
£3. 7. 6. and five Five pound notes	35	7	6
Proceeds of sale of furniture etc. less bill			
owing by Henry Hird (Shoe Harry)	5	15	6
Debt owing by James Hepburn	70	0	0
Interest received thereon	3	14	8
Debt owing by John Russell	35	0	0
Interest thereon to 14th Feb	1	8	0
Joseph Hartley	10	0	0
Interest to same date		8	0
John Hartley	60	0	0
Interest to same date	2	6	0
Joel Park	5	0	0
Interest to same date		4	0
Joseph Stilling	200	0	0
Interest to 6th January 1855	6	17	6
Box containing some old clothes and six			
silver spoons in possession of Edward Hird			
worth about	1	10	0
A silver watch on deceased person sold for			
£4. 5. 0 to Henry Hird (Shoe Harry) *who has*			
never paid for it his brother Isaac			
(...writing too small to read)*£1. 0. 0*			
(crossed out) *acct.*	4	5	0

Snuff Box of common metal not worth more than	1	0	
Memorandum: the other watch found on deceased			
claimed by a person named Brown at Thornhill			
Amount of Bill against Henry Hird for furniture			
purchased by himself and also the watch not			
then paid for. This sum deducted from			
Isaac Hird's share as he released Henry Hird			
from prison without consent of the			
administrator	10	3	11
Administration Duty	28	9	11
Bank interest	97	5	3
	£2990	*0*	*3*

It is an interesting account, as from research into other families and their locations, those who borrowed money were from either the Duddon or Esk valleys, where his kinsfolk lived.

The family of his late wife received £1,452. 17. 6d and his cousins £91. 3. 11d. each. There was no mention of any cousins from his maternal side, so perhaps Isabel had been an only child. Out of the estate, a headstone was bought. It reads:-

> *Sacred to the Memory of William Hird*   (Wm.[3])
> *Of*
> *Hollinhead in this parish who died*
> *10th June 1839 aged 75 years*
> *Also of*
> *Isabell his wife who died at Kirkby*
> *Ireleth on July 16th 1800 aged 34 years*
> *Also of Henry Hird their only son who for many*   (Hy.[3])
> *years was a resident at Thornhill in co. Dumfries*
> *who died without surviving issue at Whitehaven*
> *in this county on 27th August 1854 aged 68 years*
> *Also of Janet his wife who died at Thornhill on*
> *December 30th 1853 aged 84 years*

Reading the above, in the peace and quiet of St Catherine's church-yard in Eskdale, no one would dream of the legal battles that surrounded it.

Funerals and Funeral Customs

Death seemed to be taken for granted in olden days and funerals were big events. People often left instructions in their wills, about various things they would like done. Usually they just stated that they would like to be buried in *'Decent & Christian Manner'* in a particular Church or Churchyard and all duties and Funeral Expenses discharged. In 1596 Nicholas Wasdale of Wasdale Head stated he wished to be buried in the Church at Eskdale and in 1627 William Woodend of Arnaby in Millom stated the exact location, *'....and my body to be buried in the churchyard of Millom at the end of the Quire'* (sic). In 1768 William Wilson of Whitehaven, mariner, left nothing to chance, *'...my body to the earth or sea as it shall happen.'*

The cost of a funeral varied according to status, and, in the 17c the cost was anything from 14s. to £11.5s. In 1670, Henry Hird of Greenhead in Grasmere left estate valued at £14 and his funeral expenses were just fourteen shillings; in 1692 William Satterthwaite of Birdhow, in Little Langdale, had estate valued at £248 with funeral expenses £11.5s and two years later, Robert Satterthwaite of Fell Foot in Little Langdale whose estate was rather less at £171 had funeral expenses of £6.

In 1667, to help the wool trade, an act was passed, decreeing that all burials should be in a woollen shroud with an affidavit made to that effect at each burial, otherwise a fine was payable. The 'better off' paid the fine and buried their dead in linen. This act was gradually ignored and finally abolished in 1814.

In 1694 a Registration tax was levied on all births, marriages and deaths recorded in the Parish Registers. The Act required a complete enumeration of the population as it stood in 1695 and a tax was also levied on all bachelors over the age of twenty-five years and on all childless widowers. There was a scale of tax, again according to status, but the burial fee was four shillings, with persons on parish relief exempt.
There are not many parishes with surviving records of this tax, but one or two for Westmorland are available at the County Record Office.

Bridgett Hudleston of Millom Castle in about 1700, recorded in her account book some of the items dealing with her uncle's death and funeral, including:
'Jane Dawson for waking my uncle.'
The cost of his coffin was five shillings. Gloves were an important feature of mourning apparel and, for the above funeral, twenty-one pairs were purchased.

Quite often mourning rings were given or brooches which often contained some of the deceased's hair.

I have seen in a will '....(name given)...*to mind me when I'm dead.'*

Most parishes had a Bier on which the corpse was carried, but in some places eg. Wasdale Head, where all burials were at Eskdale, the corpse would be taken on horseback over the 'tops' along the Corpse Road. In later years the Bier was replaced with the Parish Hearse.

Funerals were gatherings of all relatives, friends and neighbours who were invited or 'Bidden' to attend. A man would be asked to go to each house and bid so many to attend the funeral, he usually received a wee drink so at the end of his journey he was quite, if not very, merry! In Victorian times, black edged Funeral Cards were sent to members of the family who were too far distant to be bid. Bidding continued into this century. Also, when a parishioner died, the church bell would toll, so many times for a man, so many for a woman and so many for a child. Different place had different numbers. This custom died out at the start of World War Two.

There always seemed to be plenty of alcohol at funerals, John Casson[7] of Sella in Dunnerdale, in his will of 1744 ... *'and it is my mind & will that my Executor or Executrix give to every Man or Woman three pence a piece, who are invited to my Funeral, to be spent at such places as I have directed my servant Alice Dawson.'* In other words he indicated in which Ale House it was to be spent. As folks travelled many miles to attend a funeral, they had to be fed, so large quantities of food were prepared. John Nicholson of Randlehow in Eskdale prepared in case it wasn't all eaten, for in his will of 1766 '.....to his widow .... *also all the provisions and eatables sparing and remaining after my funeral'*!

Mary Hird of Moorhouse supplied the food for the funeral of William Sawrey; on the next page is the account presented to the Executors.

30th October 1840.	£	s	d
2 Stones of Meal		5	0
3 Stones of Flour 9s. ½ Stone of Sugar		14	10
Loaf Sugar 1/9 Cinamon 6d Pepper d		2	4
Nutmeg 4d Tea 1s/4½d Green Tea 11d		2	7½
Tobacca and Pipes		1	2
24½ lbs cheese at 7½d		15	3
9 yards Calico 3/0s 2½yards of Print 1/3		4	3
4 lbs cheese at 7½d		2	6

Nov. 2nd
2 Stone of Meal 4/4d Candles 7d	4	11

Nov. 18 More Cheese to the value of	2	2

	£ 2	15	7½

Signed Mary Hird

Most people would walk to funerals, but the report in the Cumberland Pacquet of February 28th 1808 gives a wonderful description of a Lakeland funeral:

'Wednesday last at Eskatt in Ennerdale, Henry the only son of Mr. Henry Westray of that place, aged 30 years and greatly respected by all who knew him. His remains were interred on Friday at Ennerdale Chapel. Previously to which (according to the Custom of the neighbourhood) upwards of 150 people dined at Eskatt. In the funeral procession, which was very numerous, there were more that forty people on horseback.'

Arval bread was distributed amongst the mourners to eat on the journey home. From the bill presented by Mary Hird for William Sawrey's funeral, cheese must have been the main ingredient, but as the years went by 'ham & teacakes' were the usual fare, with of course, currant pasty and apple squares, the latter always served with cheese. There is an old saying 'Apple pasty without cheese, is like a kiss without a squeeze'.

Perhaps the longest journey to a funeral, was to that of Agnes Jackson of Cannon Street London in 1785, who, before her marriage, was Agnes Atkinson of Howe, Applethwaite. She wished to be buried with as little expense as her executor could arrange, but she '... *Desired that a horse & Mourning Coach be provided to bring down and take back.....'* some of her relatives living in Westmorland!.

In country places, people did not like to see a sparsely attended funeral, so, even if the deceased was a pauper or had no kith or kin, many would attend. In some places the bellman was sent out to announce such a death and bid folk to attend.

This was told to me many years ago, to take with a pinch of salt; "the old man was upstairs in bed dying and his wife went up to see how he was progressing. Downstairs there was great activity getting things ready. "What's that lovely smell Mary?" to which Mary replied "Thee get on wi' thee deeing, it's ham for tha Funeral Tea!"

Pitfalls for Family Historians

I would like to point out some of the pitfalls that family Historians encounter. The late Rev. B.S. Wignal Simpson, for many years vicar of Ulpha, author of *'Dale Larnin'* and *'A Mountain Chapelry'*, gave me his manuscripts and the notes he had used in their writing. Amongst these is a reference to Land Tax paid by Henry Hird, blacksmith, of Crook, Ulpha and the date 1766. This caused me much confusion and it was not until many years later, when the Vestry accounts had been deposited in the County Record Office, Barrow-in-Furness and I was able to look myself, that I found the page referred to was a loose one, with no date and written in an entirely different handwriting from the pages before and after. Turning to the next century, I found the same handwriting, thus assuring me it referred to Henry[2] born in 1769.

STEPHENSON ANCESTORS

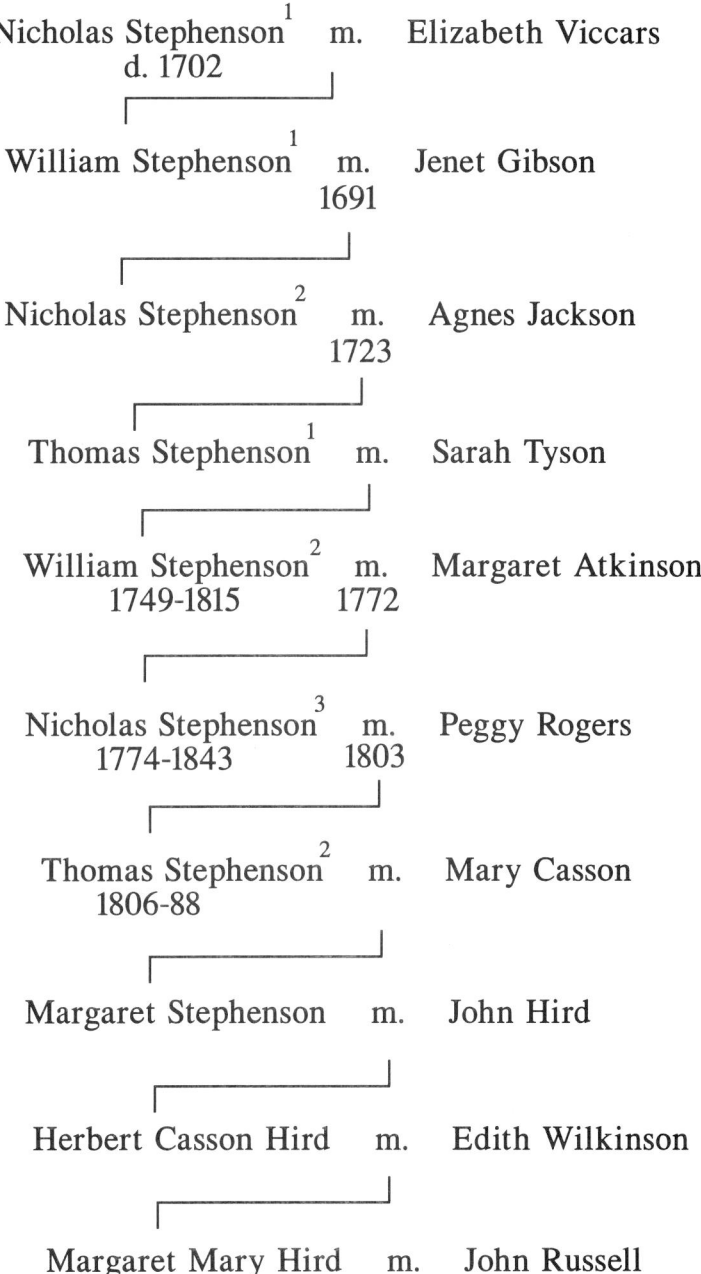

Nicholas Stephenson[1]   m.   Elizabeth Viccars
                 d. 1702

William Stephenson[1]   m.   Jenet Gibson
                      1691

Nicholas Stephenson[2]   m.   Agnes Jackson
                        1723

Thomas Stephenson[1]   m.   Sarah Tyson

William Stephenson[2]   m.   Margaret Atkinson
     1749-1815   1772

Nicholas Stephenson[3]   m.   Peggy Rogers
     1774-1843   1803

Thomas Stephenson[2]   m.   Mary Casson
     1806-88

Margaret Stephenson   m.   John Hird

Herbert Casson Hird   m.   Edith Wilkinson

Margaret Mary Hird   m.   John Russell

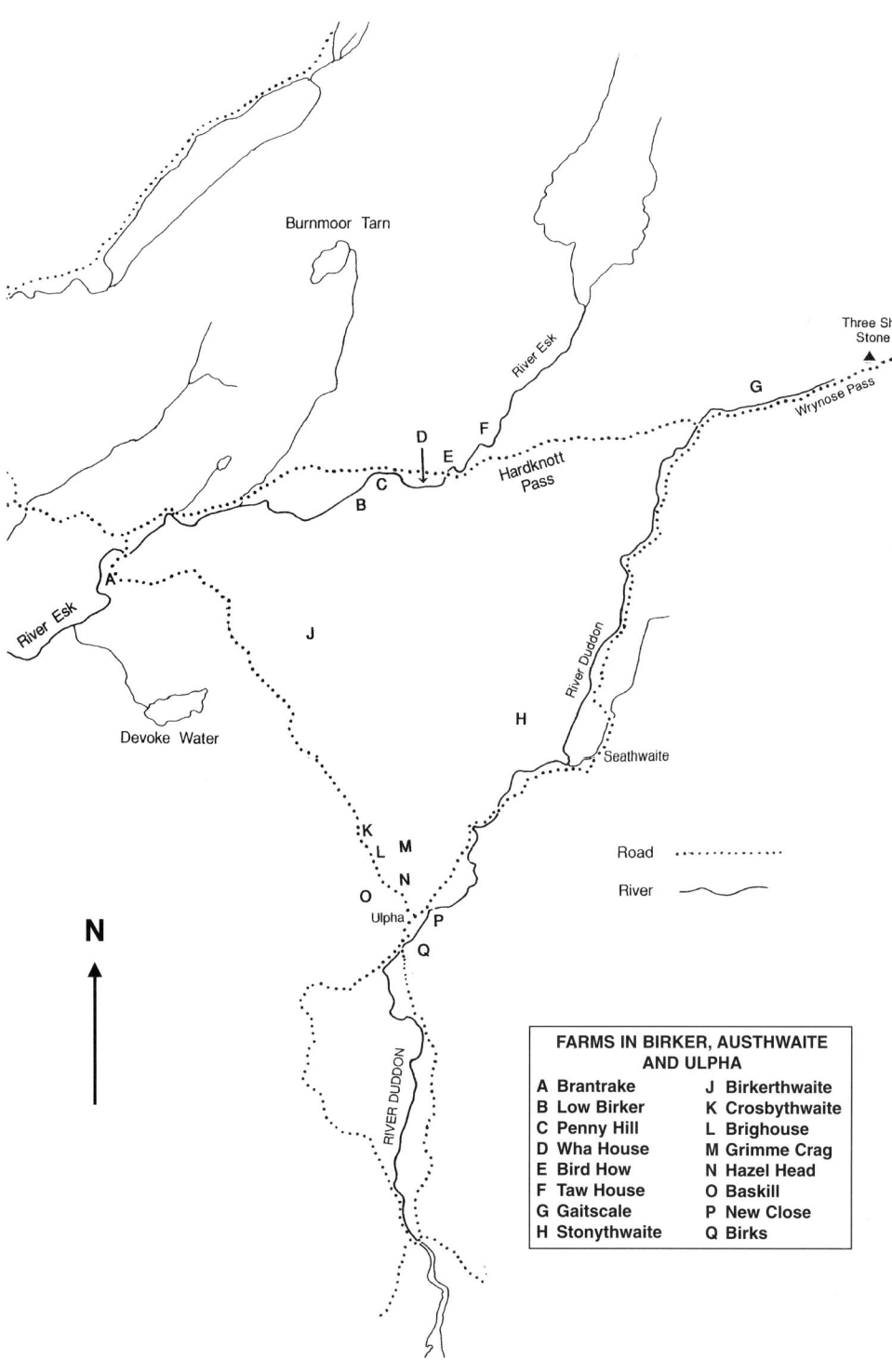

Burnmoor Tarn

River Esk

Three Shire
Stone ▲

G

Wrynose Pass

D
E
F

Hardknott
Pass

C

B

River Esk

A

J

River Duddon

H

Seathwaite

Devoke Water

K

M

L

N

O

Ulpha

P

Q

RIVER DUDDON

Road ·········

River ⌇

N

**FARMS IN BIRKER, AUSTHWAITE
AND ULPHA**

A Brantrake   J Birkerthwaite
B Low Birker   K Crosbythwaite
C Penny Hill   L Brighouse
D Wha House   M Grimme Crag
E Bird How   N Hazel Head
F Taw House   O Baskill
G Gaitscale   P New Close
H Stonythwaite   Q Birks

PART 2 - THE STEPHENSONS

Stephenson Ancestors

My paternal grandmother, Margaret Hird, was the daughter of
Thomas Stephenson and Mary Casson, she married John Hird in 1867
and produced a large family, of which my father, Herbert Casson
Hird, was the youngest child.

Early Years. References to the Name and some Local History

Stephenson is a much more common surname in the North of England than is Hird, and Cumbria, as it is today, had many families of
that name. I have found a number of early references to this name, in
a variety of documents, study of which throws interesting light on
life in West Cumberland.

The earliest reference I have to the name is in *The Commonplace
Book of Sir John Pennington 1493 - 1511* [Ms. D/Pen/200, transcript in
Record Office, Barrow.] Sir John, who died in 1512, was High Sheriff
of Cumberland from 1510 and was succeded by his son, also Sir John,
who died in 1516. (Cumberland Families & Heraldry) This is a book
which was started before Columbus discovered America, when the
main port on the south coast of Cumberland was Ravenglass and a
large part of the area would be forest.

Sir John was a rich man and also kept meticulous records as can be
seen by his Commonplace Book. In this book, he refers to selling XX
lambs to Nicholas Stephenson of Myterdalehead; this is the family
from which I am descended. He also refers to *'sheep pastures at
Birks and Gaittescale in the Duddon Valley.'* Gaitscale is now in
ruins. The sheep, which went with the place, were reputed to have an
extra rib! Birks is still habitable today. These two places would be
where the shepherds lived, one Dawson at the former and one Tyson
at the latter.

In a copy of a Deed (Ref. L331 Manchester Ref. Library) enrolled
on the Close Roll being the Will of Sir John Pennington Kt. Dated 4[th.]
May 1505, concerning his manors in Lancashire, Cumberland and
Wesmorland there is reference to the Manor of Tilberthwaite. We
were then still a Catholic Country so it is interesting to see that this
deed was witnessed by *Alexander Bank, Abbot of Furness; Robert
Chamber, Abbot of Holme Coltrum; John Bowthorn, Abbot of Cal-
der; Simond Sevus, Prior of Carlyll; Edmond Thornton, Prior of St.
Bees.'* These witnesses were from a wide area, did they make a special journey to sign this document?

The next mention of Nicholas Stevynson (sic) is in the Manorial Court Roll (D/Lec/299) where he is described as a juror and *'a Tenant at Will'* in 1523/4. He was also presented at the court by the foresters, for his cattle *'leaping over the Lord's fence'* and fined two pence.

While searching the Pennington Papers (Bundle 1) I came across a document dated 1561 which shows the movement of persons even from remote areas like Mitredale at this early date
Dated May 10th1561, it is the *'Bargain and Sale by William Jackson Citizen and Clotheworker of London and John Nicholson of Whetstone* (a London suburb), *smith, son of John Nicholson of Mytredale, of Parkhouse in Moncaster.'* (sic).
One wonders how long these two had lived in London, whether they witnessed the Coronation of Elizabeth I two years earlier or were aware of the execution of the deprived churchmen? Three years after their Bargain and Sale, Shakespeare was born. The odds are they would both be dead before his works received any recognition.

A copy of the Homerston Survey for Myterdale (1569) gives both Nicholas Stephenson sen. and Nicholas Stephenson jun. as jurors.

At the time of the Percy Survey (1578), of the nine tenements in Mytredale, five were held by Nicholsons, two by Porters, with Nicholas Stephenson and Nicholas Hartley each one.

The 'Eskdale Twenty Four Book' of 1587 mentions William Stephenson. The Twenty Four Book contains the routes by which each tenant of Eskdale had to drive their sheep up to the common pasture. It was drawn up by twenty-four tenants. Most Manors had such a book, but few have survived.

EDWARD STABLES, New Field.
Cropped near ear, key bitted both sides of the far ear,
a pop at the tail head, and a stroke from the shoulder
blade to the hock bone on the near side.

(from Hodgson *'Shepherd's Guide'* 1849)

Social History

Not all of the population of Cumberland were sheep farmers, however. Cumberland is a coastal county. In 1565 a Royal Warrant was
issued to the Lord Keeper to *'direct commissions under the Great
Seal to fit persons in each maritime county'* (State Papers Dom. Eliz.)
from this we get some idea of the local history of this period, e.g.
Whitehaven is described as having *'six houses and one vessell called a
'Pickerde'* (a large sailing boat) *tonage 9 tonnes, called the 'Bee',
used to trade herrings & killings* (codlings) *at Liverpool and Chester
and buy Salt.'* This was to supplement that produced locally from the
salt pans along the Cumberland coast. Meat and fish had to be salted
for winter as most cattle had to be killed off in the autumn.

Ravenglass boasted *Ten houses and four vessels of nine or ten
tonnes* trading as did those of Whitehaven. There were no mariners
to undertake these voyages, just fishermen. The area seemed to be
sparsely populated.

Early ancestors

The earliest document I have found with detailed information about my Stephenson ancestors is the Will of Humphrey Stevenson, merchant, proved in 1613. and it is from this that I have been able to compile the first tree.

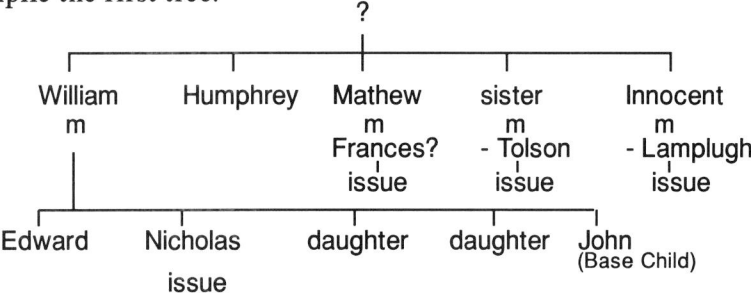

It is possible that Humphrey had another sister, as amongst his bequests is money and clothing to three sons of Robert Atkinson of Newbiggin, Westmorland, deceased. He names his niece *'Mistress Anne Tolson'* and leaves her *'forty shillings to make a Farthingale.'*

It is a will full of names and places. Humphrey Stevenson had interests at Cockermouth, even though his home appeared to be in Muncaster. Inventories were taken at both places. No name of his residence is given but the Stephensons were connected with a place called *'Yoadepark in Muncaster'*. Today there is no trace of it either as a ruin or on any early maps, yet it is mentioned in manorial papers in the late 17c. There is a crag on the right side of the road over Birker Moor on the way to Crosbythwaite, called Yoadcastle, but I would think this is too high for there to have been a dwelling.

The *Fine Book for Mytredale, 1617* (D/Lec/299) shows Nicholas Stephenson being admitted to a tenement after the death of William his father, at a yearly rent of 6s.4d. He was again admitted in 1633, following the death of the Earl of Northumberland.

In the year 1654, Robert, son of Nicholas Stephenson, took two tenements, one surrendered by William Nicholson and the other by Nicholas Stephenson, (probably his father). There is a clause, that the out Parlour of both places be used by Nicholas Stephenson and Jenet his wife for the longest life of them. In 1656 Robert Stephenson surrendered to another Nicholas Stephenson, probably his son, two tenements.

This was the Commonwealth period and times in Cumberland were not easy. It is a time when both marriages and wills are not always available and we have to rely on, and be thankful for, William Thomson, of Thornflatt, Justice of the Peace for Cumberland, from whose note-book, extracts were published in the Cumb. & West. A. & A Transactions 1914. Thomson not only conducted marriages, but also presented wrongdoers to the courts. An entry among the *'Convictions & Miscellaneous Entries', 17ᵗʰ· January 1658* (page 137, should you be able to find the original), reads:-

'On September the 14ᵗʰ 1657 were twelve men of Muncaster and other parishes convicted before me for drinking in Ulpha on the Lord's day and execution made stocking them.'

I wonder if any of the Stephensons were among the culprits and where were the stocks that they were put in?

Crosbythwaite

Crosbythwaite

Crosbythwaite is first mentioned in the Court Rolls of the Manor of Ulpha, which was within the Seigniory of Millom, in 1518, when Nicholas Sharpe took a fourth part and paid Gressum of £1.6.8d.

In the 31st Year of the Reign of Elizabeth I, (1589) Leonard Muncaster appeared against John Lewthwaite of Crosbythwaite in a plea of debt for 6s.8d.

At the general Fine of 1628, William Sharpe and James Troughton each took a tenement there.

Crosbythwaite does not appear again in any of the fines. According to Frank Warriner in his *'History of Millom',* in 1630 a Hospital was built at Whitbeck and endowed with £400 by Henry Parke a mercer of Kendal, who was born at Whitbeck. In 1639 the trustees invested the money in an annual rent charge of £24 from William and Bridget Hudleston, to be paid out of the Scoggarbar estate and out of a messuage and tenement at Crosbythwaite, Ulpha. The Ulpha lands were discharged from payment in 1744.

Before 1685, Nicholas Stephenson had moved to Crosbythwaite in Ulpha, where the Stephenson family were to remain until 1919. It was in 1685 that Nicholas applied for, and got, a licence to sell ale, Nicholas Pritt and Thomas Dickinson standing surety for him (Manorial Records). How long there was an alehouse licence for Crosbythwaite I have not been able to discover and have found no more applications or references to it.

It appears that some Stephensons were already living in the valley; as I said earlier, it was a common name. Where did the other members of the early Mytredale Stephenson families go? In the St. Bees Registers for 1689 there is mention of the Baptism in Whitehaven (by now a prosperous port), of David son of William; from the St. Nicholas Registers we find that by 1697 there were another four families of Stephensons, Isaac, Thomas, Robert, and David all having children baptised.

Once again, Letters of Attorney give some clues; one, dated 1719, tells us that Robert Stephenson, now of Cockermouth, eldest son and heir of Thomas Stephenson of Northwich, Cheshire, was surrendering his tenement in Mitredale. Another, dated 1730, refers to James and Rebecca Stephenson, both of the City of Chester, appointing Isaac Stephenson of Cockermouth, attorney, to surrender Sword House, lying in Mytredale. I have no knowledge of Stephensons being sailors and wonder why they migrated to Cheshire.

Before going to Crosbythwaite in Ulpha, Nicholas Stephenson had married Elizabeth Viccars and had children baptised at Waberthwaite Church, which seemed to be the place used by residents of Mytredale.

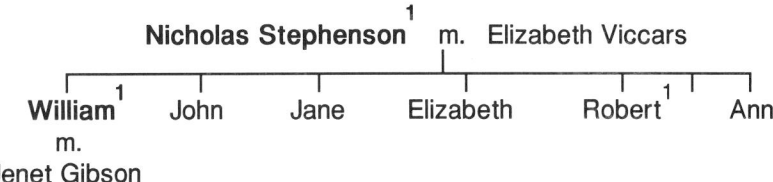

Nicholas Stephenson died in 1702. Apart from his son William, my ancestor, the only other of his children I know anything about is another son, Robert. Robert married Dorothy Sherwen, and their son, Abraham, married first Jane Nicholson at Eskdale in 1702. Abraham's only surviving issue was a son, Robert[2] who became a parson (see page 173) and died without surviving issue. So that was one Stephenson line ended.

Dorothy Sherwen's family will be mentioned again in a later section, as her sister, Jenet, married John Nicholson[4]. (page 110). Dorothy and Jenet were two of the five daughters of Thomas Sherwen of Woodhow, Nether Wasdale.

But first we must look at the family of Elizabeth Viccars.

The Viccars

There were several families of Viccars (Vickers) in Eskdale in 1569, when the Homberson Survey was taken, after the Percys lost their lands.

When the Percys lands were restored, they took a survey which shows that there were several tenements occupied by families of Viccars, all living close to each other. Elizabeth came from William the younger, of Taithes, (Tawhouse) who paid 7s.3½d. rent. With his father, William the elder, they held another tenement, the rent of which was 13s 11½d. The earliest recorded will from this family is that of William Viccars of Eskdale, dated 1592.

I think that William the younger, who died in 1661, would be Elizabeth's father. His will is interesting. He left the tenement right, as was the custom, to Thomas, his eldest son, with Elizabeth his widow to occupy it as long as she lived and kept his name. To the same son, he left ten lambs at clipping time every year for three years, the one half ewe lambs and the other half toopes (tups). Wether lambs *to the one that may be friendly to my wife and second son Henry, but he must be content with the indifferent lambs such as they will bestow upon him, I give to him twenty shillings'.* I take this as meaning the person who is helping the widow and son to execute his will. To Elizabeth his wife he left two shillings. He left to Nicholas Stevenson, younger, his son-in-law, ten shillings and to *'his wife, my daughter, two pounds of wool to be coated'* (sic?). To his two grandsons Robert and William Stevenson, one pound to Robert and two pounds to William, *'to remain in the hands of Elizabeth my wife and Henry my younger son until they come to 'perfect age'* which one presumes is twenty one years.

He then leaves money to various persons but no relationship is given, but again one presumes there must have been some family connection; *'To Robert Vickers of Wastdailehead* (sic) *To William Tyson of Wastdailehead secitor To Francis Nicholson of Padakwray* (sic) *To Elizabeth Bell To Annas Nicholson To John Wilson To John Mossop of Craighouse in Irton To Nicholas Troughtone of Craigehouse To old Richard Eilbeke in Irton To Edward Park To Edward Wilson To the wife of Thomas Tyson in Birker To Mabel Holme To William Nicholson of Longriggreen To Thomas Parker'* these people do not appear to be God children as he continues *'To every one of my Godbairns one shillings apiece.'* I began to think that perhaps the Viccars were non-conformists until I read further that he bequeathed *'Ten Shillings to the minister of Eskdale.'*

The will continues with an interesting list of possessions he was bequeathing to his younger son Henry *'All the loose boards that be about the house,* (wood was very precious as you will read further on,) *the table and forms standing in the southside of the house together with the great chaire and the great brass pot an iron* .... (undeciphable) *and a new long kist* (chest) *and two arkes* one whereof he ordained that his wife have the use of, *the bed that stands in the chamber together with the matteress, a buttoned broadcloth and cloake, a web of sadde* (sage) *greencolour my ryding saddle and a brydle.'* Chairs were not common in households at this period of time, but a 'Great Chair' must show that he was quite a man of substance and together with the tables, chests, arkes and bedstocks were valued at over £3. Wool was 7s. per stone, old sheep £4.6.8d per score and lambs £2.10s. per score. His total estate was £110.2.10d. His bequests ended with *'fourpence to Annas Tyson of Wyaos'* (Whoes).

A lot of the names mentioned above will appear futher on in this story and you will see the Viccars marrying into other lines of my family.

In his will, Thomas Viccars, who died in 1696 leaves money to William Stevenson, obviously Nicholas's son, of Crosbythwaite.

William Stephenson[1], eldest son of Nicholas[1] and Elizabeth, did not go far to find a bride, he married Jenet Gibson from the next farm, Grimme Cragg, at Ulpha Church on 17th January 1691 and fathered a large family.

The chair mentioned in this will would have been similar to this one which has been in the Casson family since the 17th century.

The Gibsons and Grimme Cragg

Anyone familiar with the Duddon Valley will know that there is no such thing as an 'isolated farmhouse' as some authors lead us to believe. All places were within earshot of one another and Grimme Crag and Crosbythwaite were no exception, together with Brighouse, Far Brighouse, Hazel Head, and two tenements at Baskell they formed a small community.

I think it is safe to say that all families in a valley in those far off days were related, and this story tells of some of the connections, some quite close, but others 6$^{th.}$ or 7$^{th.}$ cousins marrying.

An early reference to Grimme Cragg of 1622 refers to John Pratt husbandman and Jenet his natural mother of Grimme Cragg, who bargained with Thomas Casson of New Close, Dunnerdale, County Lancaster, Milner, who bought it for £20.

The Prats, Pritts or Pirts had long been in the valley. Rowland Pratt is mentioned as 'tenant at Will' in the 3rd year of Henry VIII's reign. (1511-12). In the 8th of Henry, there is reference to an admittance to Grym-cragg which was let in parts, one tenement of one quarter and one of three quarters. Richard Dixon having the small one and Richard Pirt the larger. It would appear that, when Thomas Casson bought it, the Prats (Pirts or Prits) owned both. They had been there for over one hundred years. The descendants of Thomas Casson were there over two hundred.

Thomas died in 1665 leaving a widow, Isabel, a daughter, Agnes Carter and a daughter, Margaret Casson, who, being the elder, inherited the tenement. It was well known that news of an heiress travelled fast and far, and where George Gibson came from I know not; but he married Margaret. However, according to the custom of the Manor, the property remained Margaret's as noted in the General Fines of 1688: *'Margaret wife of George Gibson was admitted Tennant of two tenements.'* She paid a General Fine of £10.

When the Lord of the Manor died and his heir took over, all tenants had to be readmitted and pay a Fine of twenty times their rent. This also applied when a tenant died, his heir had to go through the same procedure. Some times, especially when the Lord of the Manor and the Tenant died at the same time, much hardship was caused, as there was a double fine to be paid. This often led to the tenement having to be mortgaged and occasionally the place was lost.

At the time of Margaret Casson's marriage, Grimme Cragg was a prosperous farm, even if minute by today's standards.

George and Margaret raised a large family:

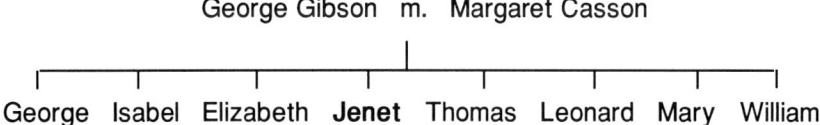

George Gibson m. Margaret Casson

George Isabel Elizabeth **Jenet** Thomas Leonard Mary William

I have very little knowledge of this family, but a document I have notes that their son Thomas went to North Scale, Walney Island and other Gibsons appear in Seathwaite at a later date.

The last Gibson to own Grimme Cragg was Mary, daughter of George, who on 24th June 1784, married John Benn, gentleman of Hestholme, Millom.

It is sad to think that a place for which the history can be traced for almost five hundred years, is now in ruins, but at least I have, in these last pages, recorded where in the Duddon Valley it was situated.

Thomas Casson was my eighth great-grandfather. More Casson ancestors in a later chapter.

More Stephensons

William Stephenson of Crosbythwaite and his wife, Jenet Gibson raised a large family, eleven children being born between 1693 and 1714.

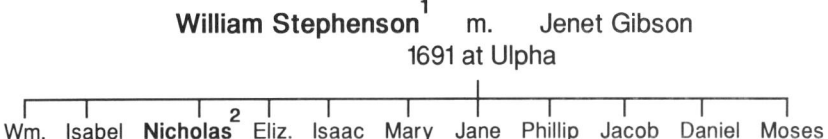

William Stephenson[1]   m.   Jenet Gibson
1691 at Ulpha

Wm. Isabel **Nicholas**[2] Eliz. Isaac Mary Jane Phillip Jacob Daniel Moses

What happened to all these children? William and Isabel both died young, as I think did Isaac as he is not mentioned in his uncle's will and Phillip died in infancy.

Jacob married Elizabeth Dennison of Baskell in Ulpha.

Elizabeth, for her second husband, married Nicholas Walker of Seathwaite.

Mary married a John Jackson of Langdale.

Jane married Edward Tyson of Penny Hill in Eskdale, (a further family link with this place).

Moses married Elizabeth Dixon of Coniston.

Daniel entered the ministry and was curate of Thwaites, where he died in 1778.

Nicholas, my direct ancestor, went to Langdale and married Agnes Jackson.

The Jacksons

Throughout the North, there are many people with the name Jackson and it is difficult to put them into families. I have not traced which family of Jacksons from Langdale that Mary Stephenson married into, but her brother Nicholas's bride was Agnes, the daughter of Henry Jackson and Jane Harrison.

Henry died in 1746 and his will describes him as *'Yeoman of William Johnson Place, Row, Wallend and lastly Thrang, Great Langdale.'* He was the son of John Jackson who was buried at Eskdale in 1702 and whose will describes him as a *Yeoman of Wasdale Head.* The family had long been settled there appearing in various surveys already mentioned. John is also mentioned in the 'Easter Book' of 1667 and again in that for 1669, (I have not inspected the one for 1668.)

'Easter Books' contain records of the Easter Offerings, ancient annual payments to the parish priest, now in general quite voluntary, but at the time I am writing about, compulsory under both common and canon law. usually exempt from the redemption of ancient obligations made under enclosure acts but commuted under the Tithe Act of 1839.

Tithes, the traditional tenth of the first fruits of the soil, varied from parish to parish and included lambs, cows, corn, hay, geese, bees, hens and various other products of the land. Wasdale Head parishioners seemed to get off lightly for their Easter Dues, paying only on *'New Milk Cows, Corn, Hay, Bees and Real ob.'* What Real stood for I do not know but could not have been of much value to have been taxed at one half penny.

[Ob is an abbreviation for obolus, a halfpenny]

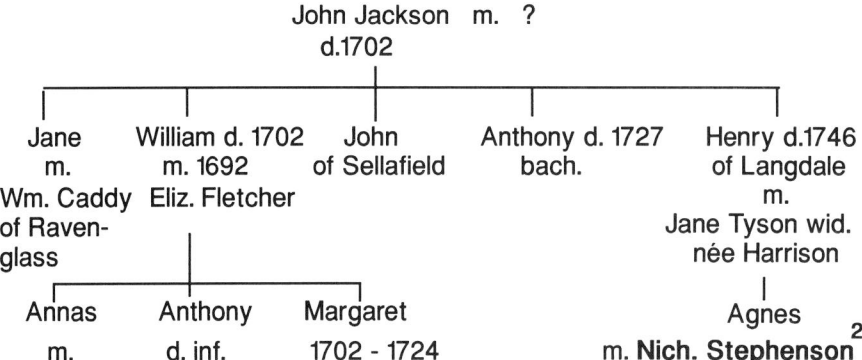

William, the eldest son, was heir to the tenement, but in 1702 tragedy struck. On 14th of April he died, leaving a pregnant widow, Elizabeth. Eight days later, his father, John, died. John had made his will just two days earlier, to assure that, if his pregnant daughter-in-law had a son, her daughter Annas should receive a legacy of three pounds, but if another girl was born, then the younger daughter was to receive the said legacy, as Annas would become heiress to the tenement. On 4th June of the same year, Elizabeth's second daughter was baptised and, on 23rd of June, just nineteen days later, Elizabeth was buried. We will never know the cause of these three deaths so close together.

Elizabeth, in her nuncupative will, made on the 17th June, asks her brothers-in-law John, Anthony and Henry Jackson to look after her children. There is no mention of her sister-in-law, Jane Caddy. Which brother undertook the task? John was at Sellafield, Henry at Langdale and Anthony was a bachelor, yet I have a feeling it was Anthony. Margaret, Annas' sister, died in 1724 and Anthony died in 1727. Although he had several other nephews and nieces, he left the bulk of his estate of £266.11s. to Annas and made her his Executrix.

As are all inventories, Anthony's was valued and appraised by four just men, John Jackson, Robert Hunter, Henry Viccars and John Tyson the latter probably Annas' husband. Tradition leads us to believe that they always under rather than over valued the inventories. I would not know, what is interesting are the debts owing to Anthony.

John Sueart	£30	William Atkinson	£5
George Mackereth	£20	Robert Willson	£5
Henry Jackson	£20	Jane Caddy	£3
Samuel Birkett	£10	William Sherwen	£1
John Brag	£10	John Dixon	£1

Sueart, and Mackereth are both Westmorland names and Birkett and Dixon are names associated with both Cumberland and Westmorland. My guess is that the money they owed was for wool, which would have been transported from Wasdale Head and sold, probably in Kendal, having been taken by packhorses over Styhead, down through Great Langdale to Kendal. Was it on such a mission that Henry Jackson met widow Jane Tyson née Harrison?

No research has been done on Jane, she may have been one of the same family as William Harrison accused of the murder of William Dixon (page 15).

From her first marriage to Thomas Tyson of William Johnson Place, Jane had two children, William and Elizabeth and from her marriage to Henry Jackson, the following six children.

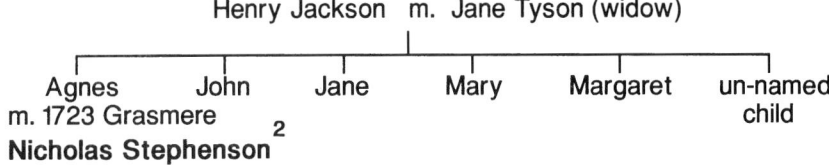

Henry Jackson   m.   Jane Tyson (widow)

Agnes	John	Jane	Mary	Margaret	un-named
m. 1723 Grasmere					child
Nicholas Stephenson[2]					

Wastwater

More Stephensons

Little is known about the early years of Nicholas and Agnes's marriage. William, their first child, was baptised at Ulpha, with Henry, Jane and Mary at Grasmere, where their father was described as '*of Rossett*'. Thomas's baptism I have not found. It is possible that Nicholas farmed at Cleator for a while.

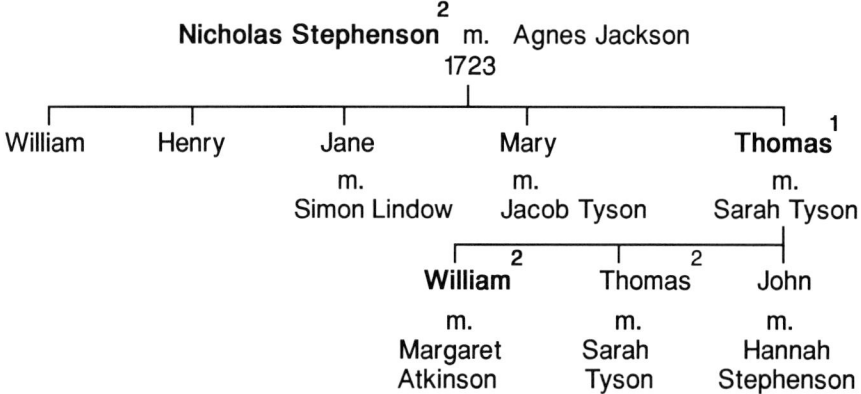

William and Henry must have died young, as there is no mention of them in the wills of either their father or uncle, the Rev. Daniel Stephenson. Both daughters married young men from Cleator, Mary being united with Jacob Tyson, (more about her later), and Jane with Simon Lindow. Not much is known about this latter marriage. Thomas, my ancestor, eventually inherited Crosbythwaite.

Contrary to the custom and despite being the eldest son, Nicholas Stephenson does not appear to have inherited Crosbythwaite. It belonged to his brother, the Rev. Daniel. Whether he bought it from his father or it was conveyed to him, as sometimes tenancies were, I do not know, I quote from the Rev. Daniel's will;

'.... *unto my nephew Thomas Stephenson, my farmer, all my Freehold Estate at Crosbythwaite in Ulpha in the parish of Millom and County of Cumberland, together with all other freehold Land whatsoever within the parish of Millom to hold to him the said Thomas Stephenson his heirs and assigns for ever.*'

Daniel mentioned all his many nephews and nieces, a wonderful will for compiling family trees. There is one noticeable omission, he did not leave anything to the poor of Thwaites of which parish he had been curate for almost forty years. Perhaps he thought his family more in need!

Thomas, as you can see from the tree on the previous page, married Sarah Tyson, who bore him three sons, William, Thomas and John. Sadly, she died quite young.

William[3], my ancestor, married Margaret Atkinson in 1772 and produced a large family (more about the Atkinsons in a later chapter).

Thomas[2] entered the Church; he married a Sarah Tyson who was a niece of his brother William's wife. (see p. 155)

John became a maltster at Broughton and married in Liverpool, his wife being Hannah Stephenson of Seathwaite, no relation as far as is known.

An Eighteenth Century Spice Cupboard

Social History

Today, as we travel along the country roads, we pass over the rivers and streams by good, well built bridges, many widened this century to accommodate today's transport, but bridges have been in existence for centuries. As early as 1531 there was a Statute of Bridges. County Quarter Sessions were empowered to appoint two bridge surveyors within the area and level a rate of maintenance of bridges and the highways for 300 yards of either side of them. Most counties did not appoint surveyors at this time, the usual arrangement being that one or more local Justices of the Peace supervised the work of the county bridge repair and recouped their expenses at the next session. In Cumberland the first *'Bridge Surveyor or Planner'* was appointed at the Midsummer sessions 1775.

There is much useful information for the Family or Historical researcher amongst the Quarter Sessions Indexes (Record Office, Carlisle) such as deeds, bonds, petitions for repairs and the building of a bridge.

e.g. *'1751 Edward Tyson and Thomas Tyson of Brantrake, yeomen, John Pearson Howhouse, in Muncaster, John Vicars of How, in Millom,* (Austhwaite was in the parish of Millom) presented a petition by the Inhabitants of Austhwaite and Eskdale, setting forth that the road from Austhwaitefield to Eskdale , *'is become a great Thoroughfare'* and that the ford over the river Esk at Stonepott is frequently very *'Dangerous and impassable, some having perished therein and several been in great danger and people are often obliged to go another way and that a stone bridge at Stonepott near the said ford on a Moderate Estimate will cost Fifty Pounds.'*

Petitions for repairing bridges: in 1691 at the Epiphany Sessions such a one from the parishioners of Egremont, Beckermont, Haile, Ponsonby, Gosforth, Irton, Drigg and Muncaster for the rebuilding of Street Bridge over the river Kirkbeck on the road from Whitehaven and Egremont to Lancaster and Kendal, adding that several had drowned there. It was signed by 25 persons. In 1703 'Great Land Floods' occurred, one on the 14[th.] of August and another on the 19[th.] of September which washed away many bridges. The residents petitioned at the Quarter Sessions for money to rebuild them. One casualty was that bridge called Nettleslack in Seathwaite and a petition to restore it, with fifty names, can be seen in the Lancashire R.O. Preston (QSP 902/9). Some of the fifty signed with a mark but thirty three were able to sign their name. It is often wrongly assumed that, at this time most people were illiterate.

Floods seemed to be frequent events, especially in August, as there is, in 1713, an agreement between Sir William Pennington of Muncaster, Bart., Edward Stanley of Dalegarth, John Ponsonby of Haile on one part and James Lancaster, carpenter, of Muncaster and John Hunter of Irton, for *'setting forth that bridge called Cleator Bridge & part of the Causway which were lately driven down by a violent flood which fell in August last'* and also Longbridge at Hardknott foot. There is a bond showing that they also rebuilt Cleator Great Bridge, Ewart Bridge and Egremont Bridge.

There is a document in which states that in 1786 *'Thomas Stephenson of Crosbythwaite in Ulpha Yeoman, was held & firmly bound unto George Gibson of Grimme Cragg, Yeoman in the sum of fifty pounds of good & Lawful money of Great Britain* (etc.) ..... *whereas on the nineteenth day of July last past the said George Gibson did contract & agree with the said Thomas Stephenson for the building of a Bridge over the Gill at Crosbythwaite for the sum of Ten Pounds to be finished & completed before the Twenty ninth Day of September and to maintain it, support, uphold and keep the same in good repair for seven years.'* The bridge which stands there today, is in good condition, is it the one that Thomas built? I like to think so.

Crosbythwaite Bridge

William Stephenson's family.

The marriage of William Stephenson and Margaret Atkinson pro-duced seven children.

William Stephenson[2] m. Margaret Atkinson
1772

Sarah	Nicholas[3]	Anthony	Ann	Daniel	Margaret	Mary
1773-1809	1774-1843	1776	1777-1840	b. 1779	1781-1855	1783
m. 1759	m. 1803	d. inf.	m. 1797		m. 1802	d. inf
Matt. Jenkinson	Peggy Rogers		James Dawson (shoemaker)		Thomas Dawson (house carpenter)	

Nicholas, my direct ancestor, was married in Eskdale to Peggy Rogers in 1803 - more about them later.

Two daughters of this family married Dawsons, both from the Dud-don Valley. Ann was married in Eskdale, but her husband, James Dawson was an Ulpha lad; Margaret married Thomas Dawson whose residence was Hall Dunnerdale, Seathwaite, he could well have been James's brother, but I have not worked out their relationship with certainty, however, I am sure there will be one.

Candlesticks from Moorhouse

The Dawsons

The Dawson family had long been settled in the Duddon Valley, certainly as far back as the end of the 16c. possibly before that, as one of Sir John Pennington's shepherds was of that name. Dawsons have married into most of the families in the valley, including those of my forebears, but I have no known direct Dawson ancestors. Oral history claims they came over from Grasmere and settled in Seathwaite, at Thrang.

One, Thomas Dawson, who died in 1778, had gone over to Grasmere to marry Margaret Fleming on 19th. February 1754. It was their son, James, who married Ann Stephenson in 1797. James and Ann had eleven children between 1798 and 1823, two of whom I have traced to Cheshire; Elizabeth, unmarried in the 1851 census and Mary, who married at Marple, Joseph Johnson. What brought them to Cheshire? While researching, I discovered others in that area by the name of Dawson, but have no idea if they too, were originally from Cumbria.

Of the other children, James, like his father, was a shoemaker, who would no doubt have travelled around the country as a journeyman. He married Elizabeth Hartley from Egremont, possibly meeting her during these travels. (One of his sisters married William Harrington, also from the Egremont area, so there seems to have been some connection with those parts.)

James Dawson and Elizabeth Hartley had an even larger family than his parents, thirteen children in all, eight sons and five daughters. They were all educated and then scattered to the far corners of the world.

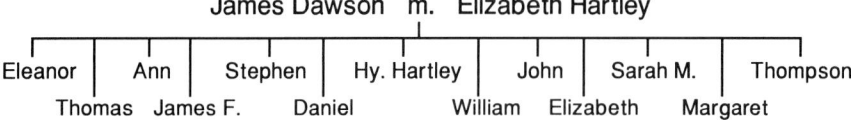

James Dawson m. Elizabeth Hartley

Eleanor	Ann	Stephen	Hy. Hartley	John	Sarah M.	Thompson
Thomas	James F.	Daniel		William	Elizabeth	Margaret

Eleanor married John Porter of Eskdale. She wrote delightful poetry (see Page 136) and it is thanks to her grandson's preservation of old family letters and her brother Thomas's conversations with me as a small girl, that a lot of their family history has been compiled.

Shortly before he died, John Porter (the grandson) sent me the following letter which he had found amongst the old papers he had preserved. He had previously loaned me a bundle of old letters and poems, which he was at that time sorting through, in connection with production of his excellent book *'94 years in Eskdale'*. The letter, to James Dawson and Elizabeth, is from her parents and it contains some social history as you will read;

> *'Haggatend (Egremont) January 20th. 1839* (spelling as written)
> *Dear Son & Daughter,*
> *I take this Oportunity of writing to you hoping you are all in good health at present we wish to know how you are coming on after this 'hurricane' as we have had our palour and shop windows blown in and our Barn has been removed of a quantity of Slates. The Mill at Bridge end has also ...oved considerly. Joseph & Elizabeth continues much the same that young man the name of Hugh Develin was drowned in the harbour of Cardiff in Wailes* (sic) *about a fortnight ago, a young woman the name of Mary Anderson of Egremont was killed by a chimney blowing down Abraham & Henry & families are all in good health and Abraham expects his Family increasing every day. Please to give our best respects to your Father & Mother* (James Dawson and Ann, née Stephenson) *and if you will wright when you are 'confined' I intend to come over. We have nothing more particular to say   So we remain yours Etc*
> *   Henry & Eleanor Hartley'*

A brief but a very informative letter. Research shows that Elizabeth had already been confined of a son, his name was Thomas, the wonderful gentleman to whom I owe so much.

Another letter that has survived was written in 1862 by father James Dawson, to, I assume, his sister Elizabeth, in Cheshire. This shows that he too was an enterprising man. At the age of 58 years he sat down to write .... I quote (there are very few punctuations) *'a hurried scrawl as I have very little time to write I think less than usual as I have engaged a new line of Business I have commenced trying to 'teach the idea how to shoot' but I am not determined whether I shall continue it or not it will not be sufficient for a living but if I can make it do with the Clerk and Overseer place and working at nights and Saturdays Thos and Stephen are quite fit to carry on the Business at Home. The trustees for Ulpha were obliged to offer it to the Clergyman and if he refused it to appoint a New one and he fearing the appointment of a person not agreeable to himself accepted it and employs me as his Usher and he superintends occasionlly. We have been at work three weeks. I like it well enough but am rather too far off but if I continue I must have a Bed and not come constantly home, Danl. has gone to John Atkinson to be a joiner the other man dismissed on account of his deafness, Fleming is here he came last night to make a suit of clothes for himself I expect not to be at much expence on his account as his Master will have to give him a suit next year'* (He will then have finished his apprenticeship and the Master gave each apprentice a suit.) *'Sickness and death have been prevalent all through the Country not particularly in this neighbour but the Country round there has been a kind of bad cold which few have escaped.* He continues with baby Thompson's health, then news of Hartley who continues with T. Dawson, who prizes him highly. He finishes with *...we have not seen M. A. Harrington yet I have to go to Ravenglass to pay the Income Tax for Ulpha and intent to go there all night as Thomas has made three pairs of Wellington Boots for them.*

    Affectionately etc   Jas Dawson'

James was educated, but where? Most vicars taught the village children if their parents desired, so most children received some tuition.

Another letter which shows the interest in his surrounding countryside was written on January 15th 1896 by Thomas Dawson (b. 1839) describing a walk he had taken a couple of days earlier as it was a *'nice fine day'.* He had gone to the Roman Fort on Hardknott to explore it, but while there had memorised the houses and farms at the top end of the Eskdale valley and when he returned home, learned their names. He refers to the excavations, and an interview Robert Sawrey had with the foreman - the latest discovery was a lot of bones, there were large ones and small ones and thought to be the remains of a cat and kittens. He ended the letter with *'Mrs S. of Crosbythwaite has presented her Lord and Master with a fifth daughter!'* The 'Lord & Master' was my great uncle.

The Robert Sawrey mentioned, lived at Stoneythwaite. A lovely story about him was told by my aunt: as his teeth dropped out he carefully placed them in a small tin. It was his wish that they were to be buried with him. Every time my grandmother and aunt visited, Robert proudly exhibited his teeth!

To return to the large family of Dawsons, children of James and Elizabeth; John went to Canada or America, as did Elizabeth after she married a Scotsman, James Phimister. Stephen was working in London and Hartley and Thompson went to New Zealand. There are many letters, all of them interesting, but space does not allow them all to be printed, so I have chosen the one describing Hartley's arrival in New Zealand at a time when many Cumbrians were emigrating.

'Exeter House, Mc.Laggan Street,Dunedin, N.Z. 16th. Dec 1878
Dear Mother, Brother & Sisters,
   6.20 p.m the Sun shining brightly. A gentle breeze blowing from
the East. I have returned from work and had my tea; it is now seven
in the morning with you, as dark as pitch (unless you have the moon),
so you see I have gained nearly a day's march on you and am getting a
summer in advance. The Letter Box for the next British Mail closes
here on 20ᵗʰ so I thought I had better get ready for it though you will
miss my report of Xmas here this time.
   I will now continue my account of our voyage from where I left
off in my last note. We started away from Melbourne on the 20ᵗʰ No-
vember about 4pm with a full ship of cargo and passengers mostly
British and half a dozen Chinamen. We (Steerage) had plenty of
room on deck in this boat but were too closely packed below. I slept
on deck one fine night and very pleasant it was. We had first rate
provisions and plenty of them. I was slightly sick the day after we
sailed. This boat had a different motion to the Cuzco. We had a nice
passage with a favourable wind all the way more or less two or three
days pretty rough. On Monday 25ᵗʰ about 3.30pm we sighted the land
of our adoption.
   As it became more distinct, as far as we could see land, the hills
rose to an immense height an abundance of peaks caped with snow,
(not unlike winter at home) like a gathering of venerable hoary
headed giants sitting in council. On sighting land we slackened so as
to be able to run into the Bluff Harbour at day light in the morning
as we could not reach it before dark and the ships cannot go in at
night. Shortly after 6am on the 26ᵗʰ we ran along side the pier at
Bluff and remained until 5pm. We immediately went on shore but
shortly returned for breakfast.
   There are not many houses, they are built of wood. The Harbour is
a fine spacious one rather shallow at some places: it is sheltered by
the Western Hills. Land about is chiefly in its natural wild state and
fine and romantic does it look. Moist places growing flax, the dry
places and ravines covered with a variety of trees; in some places so
densely interwoven as to be impenetratable; at other places some of
the trees are lying in a variety of forms, just as they had been up-
rooted or blown down by the wind and perhaps remained for centur-
ies. I ascended a hill, where the pilot signals are, from which there is
a fine outlook away in the direction of Invercargill, and as far south
as the coast. The country is very level for a distance back of perhaps
20 miles; then rise the eternally snow capped mountains. Stewert Isle
lies to the south, which is also very hilly. The people here (Bluff) are
mainly employed in shipping and about the harbour; all I saw were
British (at least European). At 5pm we steamed away again, and at
daybreak on the 27ᵗʰ we sailed past Dunedin, round the entrance of
Port Otago and arrived at port Chalmers about 7am and so our voy-

*age is completed in just two calander months from embarking to
disembarking minus one day.'*

He then took a train to Dunedin the journey and the place he describes and continues with his narrative: *'On leaving the Railway
Station I was to look out for the Bank of N.Z. which I espied and
entered was detained there some time. I then resolved to at once
canvas for a job, and succeeded in getting one early in the afternoon
at the N.Z. Colonial Wood Ware Factories in the name of Guthrie and
Larnach, but I am told it has a good many shareholders. It is a large
concern; in fact they claim to have the largest business in the wood-
line, out of Britain or America. It consists in Carpentry, Cabinet
Work, Upholstery, Coopering, Waggon Work, Glaziery, Timber
Merchants, Turning, and almost any sort of Ironmongery. They have
the most and best machinery of any place that I have wrought at. I
did not expect to meet with a place like this in the Colony at all
events.*

*When I asked the foreman for a job, at first he said 'No', then he
asked me where I had been working. I said I had just arrived from
the Old Country, he asked me what ship I had come in: I replied that
I had come by the S.S. Cuzco to Melbourne thence by the the S.S.
Albion, and that I had worked in London, Manchester and Glasgow.
He then asked if I came from Wales (the old duffer to take me for a
Welshman), I answered with some dignity 'No Sir, I am an English-
man, I belong to the North of England' he then said I could start,
'but' he said 'we do not pay full money to strangers until they get
accustomed to our ways'. I thought this reasonable enough so I accepted the job and departed to look for lodgings.'*

These he found at 7s a week, and brought his luggage from the station. He commenced work on November 28th, his thirty-first birthday. That week he worked seventeen hours and received £1.1s.3d. He
started work at 8am, had half an hour allowed for dinner at 12 noon
and finished at 5pm except on Saturdays, when they finished at
2.00pm. He reckoned rent and provisions cost him about sixteen shillings a week, so he would be able to save twice as much money as he
could at home. He continues:

*'I have been making enquiries and am on the look out for a profitable
investment or speculations. The money it has cost me to come out
here (which indirectly will be £50) I intend shall pay me good interest. Necessaries in provisions are reasonable enough in price, it is the
luxuries that are so dear, meat is cheap; and butter, bread, tea, sugar
be pretty much the same as at home; most other things are dear,
house rent and firing included; wearing apparel is not so dear as I
expected.'*

He then describes the crops grown in the area, that sheep shearing has been going on for several weeks and that about a dozen men came on the boat with them from Melbourne for that purpose. The great variety of trees, Fuchsias being very common, but not the kind his mother used to have in a pot in the parlour window but large ones like a full grown yew at home.

He ends with: *'There are a lot of trout in the brooks, I propose trying my hand amongst them at the holidays. There is plenty of chance with gun also. I see it is a very common instrument here, I must have one got; there are pheasants, rabbits, wildpigs, a sort of parrot and I don't know what all. Ones ears catch many familiar sounds amongst the songsters too; there is the sky-lark, the blackbird, the thrush, the spink* (chaffinch) *and others all of which seem to sing as melodiously or more so than at Home.*

I made use of one of the addresses last weekend, that I received at Glasgow; the parties came out 16 years ago; they have a family of 5 living and 2 dead, all of which were born out here. The man is a cabinet maker by trade, they have a house about £400 value, but it is heavily mortgaged owing to the man drinking.

It will be about the middle of February before you get this. It will at the soonest be a good way into April before I get a note from you. I shall be expecting one about then as I shall be thirsting for news. I hope and trust you are all well and that Mother got safely back from Oldham all the better for her trip.

Yours affectionately
Hartley Dawson.'

A piece of writing one would associate more with an experienced journalist, rather than a young carpenter from a small village amongst the Lakeland hills.

He moved on to several places, and, in 1886 he bought or as he says 'took' 150 acres of land for himself and 75 for his brother Thompson at two shillings and six pence per acre (12½p.in today's money). The land was in the County of The Bay of Islands situated eight or nine miles from Kara Kara. Thompson joined him, as did their nephew Arthur Dawson. Hartley died c. 1902 as letters from his brother Thompson speak of trying to sell the farm; he had never married. Thompson had, and he and his wife ran a drapery business, unfortunately he was drowned while bathing in a pool before attending a Masonic Meeting in January 1907. At the time his wife was pregnant with twins. All contact with both Arthur and Thompson's families was lost until a few years ago, when, through these letters, they met up with each other and their English cousins. The last twin died in 1998 a lovely lady whom I met when I visited New Zealand.

From the mid 19c. many left the valleys and dales for far away places, having no fear of travel, as can be seen from another letter written on August 15[th.] 1910, by a John Dawson who gives his address as Ymire (sic) B.C. Canada. I do not think this is brother to the above because of the mention of 'Aunt Phebe'. He is writing to John Sawrey of Grass Guards.

'Dear John,
    I now take the pleasure of writing a few lines to you hoping you are all in good health as the same leaves me at present. I have got back to Canada. I stayed in Australia about 10 months. I was around the mines there but work was bad to get so I went to Queensland where Aunt Phebe is. I worked there for 5 months. I saw David Sawrey there, Robert Sawrey's nephew we were working together, he has a big family. I was working on fruit farms, it was great fun grow-ing oranges & bananas and all kinds of fruit one could mention but wages were pretty small they only paid about 5/- a day but I had a fine trip around. I was in all the principle towns in Australia, I did nothing for 5 months but travel around I came back to Canada by Pacific Ocean, I landed on the first of June I am working at the mine again and doing fine. Young Isaac Slee is working up here where I am at and he is getting along fine. It has been a very fine summer here, everything being dry some big bush fires, lots of fine timber destroyed and property. I haven't much more time so hoping to hear from you soon I will close.
    I remain your old friend
John Dawson'

The descendants of David Sawrey are still in Australia, one Bill Sa-wrey has compiled a very large index of Sawreys world wide and has visited this country on several occasions. The young Isaac Slee would be son of Isaac and Mary Agnes Slee née Tyson and grandson of the famous illicit whisky distiller Lanty Slee.

All these letters were written in a good legible hand.

Nicholas Stephenson[3] (1774-1843) and Peggy Rogers

Nicholas[3] and Peggy married from Dalegarth Hall, in Eskdale. The Rogers had appeared in Eskdale Registers in the early 18[th]c. Peggy's grandmother was Jane Pool. The Pools had taken over the tenancy of Milkinsteadmire between 1699 and 1706 when the name of William Pool appears in the list of tenants of Birker and Austhwaite. Edward Dixon was there in 1699 and there do not appear to be any surviving lists for the inbetween years.

Peggy's father, Joseph Rogers was born in 1745, the son of William Rogers and Jane Pool who were married at Eskdale in January 1739/40. Peggy's mother was Elizabeth, third daughter of John Viccars by his second wife, Elizabeth Tyson.

The first entry for this family in the parish registers is 1703 and from them I have compiled a tree, (see following page); interesting that the Christian names are different from those of the majority of the inhabitants in the area. Had they earlier been nonconformists?

Casson Stephenson, grandson of Nicholas and Peggy, was the 'Lord and Master' in the Dawson letter; he was also responsible for planting the trees on the fell side near Crosbythwaite as a shelter for his cattle. He retired in 1919 and moved to High Hurst, where he died.

His brother, Thomas[3] did not marry, so another branch of the Stephensons died out. The descendants of Moses (1714-1748), youngest son of William Stephenson[1] and Jenet Gibson, farmed at Panel Holme until the early 1900s. They have male descendants scattered far and wide but, alas, none of that name still survive in the valley.

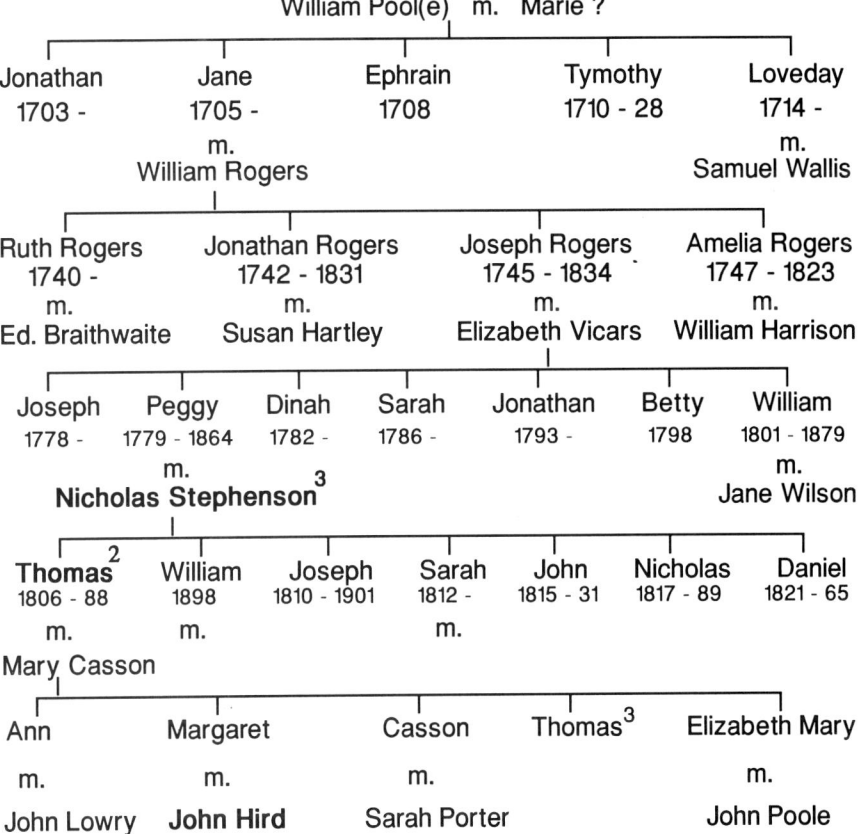

William Pool(e) m. Marie ?

Jonathan	Jane	Ephrain	Tymothy	Loveday
1703 -	1705 -	1708	1710 - 28	1714 -
	m.			m.
	William Rogers			Samuel Wallis

Ruth Rogers	Jonathan Rogers	Joseph Rogers	Amelia Rogers
1740 -	1742 - 1831	1745 - 1834	1747 - 1823
m.	m.	m.	m.
Ed. Braithwaite	Susan Hartley	Elizabeth Vicars	William Harrison

Joseph	Peggy	Dinah	Sarah	Jonathan	Betty	William
1778 -	1779 - 1864	1782 -	1786 -	1793 -	1798	1801 - 1879
	m.					m.
	Nicholas Stephenson[3]					Jane Wilson

Thomas[2]	William	Joseph	Sarah	John	Nicholas	Daniel
1806 - 88	1898	1810 - 1901	1812 -	1815 - 31	1817 - 89	1821 - 65
m.	m.		m.			
Mary Casson						

Ann	Margaret	Casson	Thomas[3]	Elizabeth Mary
m.	m.	m.		m.
John Lowry	**John Hird**	Sarah Porter		John Poole

There has survived in the family a rather remarkable book, hand written but date unknown, it contains recipes and remedies for both humans and animals, and, in a number of instances the names of those who recommended the cure. What appears to be the earliest is, and I quote (spelling as written):-

'Dr. HulstÆs Proscription of Powders to take after her Plurisy in Asses Milk. For Mrs Mary Dormer, April ye 8th. 1730 she having a Cough & being inclined to a loosness.. Take of prepared Coral one Scruple, Japan earth Six grains, of Sugar of Roses, half a Scruple, mix them and make a powder, give this quantity morning and Evening with Asses Milk.'

Or how about 'A PURGE Take an ounce of Manna disolved in a large cup of Mint water, warmed & strained, thirty grains of Glauber Salts, one dramm of Senna, two spoonfulls of Aqua Mirabilis' recommended by Dr. Frewin

For a burn or scald, Mrs Parkhurst sen, suggested beating the white of an Egg, with Alome till it comes to a froath, & lay that froath, or curd on the Burn, & as it grows dry do ye. place again with more, for 5 or 6 times.' while Dr Burrell's cure was:- 'Imediately lay Fine Cloths, wetted in rectified Spirit of Wine & keep them on, wet for 2 or 3 hours.'

What of the cures for animals? By the sound of the following, today's MOH would be horrified! 'For a Cow when she is weak & can Scarce get up when she is down & her Teeth loos & has what is called about Cheltenham 'The Worm in the Taile' Examine all along her Tail & you will find there is no Bone only a Sort of Grissel for about the length of ye Finger in some part cut the Hair off yt. place & cot it open & Lay into the wound along ye Taile when it oponed Some Rue picked from ye stalks & then pounded with Fat rusty Bacon & a Snail close it into ye wound & sow a Cloth Tite together over where it is cut and don't open it for five to ten days or more than a week be sure don't cut it cross ways or you will cut the Cows Taile off pound with ye. Rue a Clove or Two of Garlick & Fat of Some Rusty Bacon is best & no Salt & a black Snaile.'   Accredited to Giles Moor.

Social History

Birker and Austhwaite, at one time were owned by two different Lords. Both were in the Parish of Millom, being on the south of the river Esk, however their parishioners were allowed to marry in St. Catherine's Church at Eskdale, which was in the parish of St. Bees.

Birker was also, in the 17c, a stronghold for the Quakers who on January 10[th.] 1693/4 made Application at the Quarter Sessions for a Licence to hold meetings :-

'To Their Majesty's Justices of the peace Generall Easter Sessions held at Cockermouth the 10[th.] January Anno Domi. 1693/4
Humbely Sheweth that According to a late Act of Parliament made Whereas All Dissenters are required to Licence their Publice Meeting houses Wee thought it fit to request the Benifitt of the said Act and Humbely intreat you to grant us licence for these houses and which for the People Caled quakers to meet in & We shall Acknowledge it a favour done to your Friends.'

Of the two requested, Edward Tyson's house at Birkerthwaite and Joseph Leech's house at Redd-Brow in the Parish of Millom, only Edward Tyson's house received a Licence.

Birkerthwaite Meeting house is mentioned in the Will of Agnes Jackson of the Crook Ulpha, who left it £5 and wished to be buried at Newclose, the Quaker burial ground at Seathwaite. (This is still there, a peaceful place) She was probably the Agnes Dickinson, daughter of John Dickinson of Brighouse, who was married at Marsh Grange in 1677, to John Jackson of Newclose. [Soc. of Friends, M/f (Lancs Record Office) RG 6, Reel3.]

The records of the Ecclesiastical Court for 1689, that hauled Quakers, Catholics and all other dissenters before it, states that *'Edward Tyson and Annas his wife Isabell Holme, John Tyson & Isabel his wife, John Tyson & Edward Tyson'* were charged with not attending Divine Service adding *'Being Quakers'* also charged with proving a will were Briget Tyson and Jane Tyson Executrixes of John Tyson and Henry and Thomas Willson for the same thing.

. There were also Quakers, by the name of Tyson, over the hill in Ulpha, at Grassguards. This family chose to be buried at Hawkshead, rather than the burial ground at Seathwaite. This suggests that they were related to the family of Hugh and Ann Tyson of Hawkshead, the family with which Wordsworth boarded as a schoolboy; Hugh Tyson was known to have lived in the Duddon valley as a child.

The Swarthmoor Meeting house in Ulverston kept in close contact with Birkerthwaite. The minutes of a Womens Meeting in 1681 helps to piece together the sad story of Isabel Holmes:-

'This day wee have had under our Consideration the necesseity of our poor Friend Isabell Holme of Eskdale who is near her time of lieing In: Soe wee find there is need that she bee helped with something towards her Relief and her Husband is at this time a sufferer for the Testymony of Jesus against Tyths.'

Five shillings was sent to her by one Dorothy Beck. By the 4th of the following month Isabel had been delivered of 'tow' children and Friend Mary Walker was sent to Eskdale with five shillings more relief, but finding Isabel's needs were not too great, only left four. Shortly after this, word was received that Isabel's husband

'... this day a prisoner at Carlyell for truths & testymony; and now lies weake and Sicke: and has sent for his wife to come to him and shee being in a low condition & has a young child (one of the Tow must have died) *that she cannot leave behind her doeth desire some Assisstance from us; it being a considerabel Jorney'*

She received another five shillings. It is not known if Isabel got to Carlisle before her husband died, but whatever it did not lessen her faith, as you will have read, she was still being persecuted for not going to Divine Service seven years later.

Quaker Burial Ground, New Field

NICHOLSON ANCESTORS
(Slapestones)

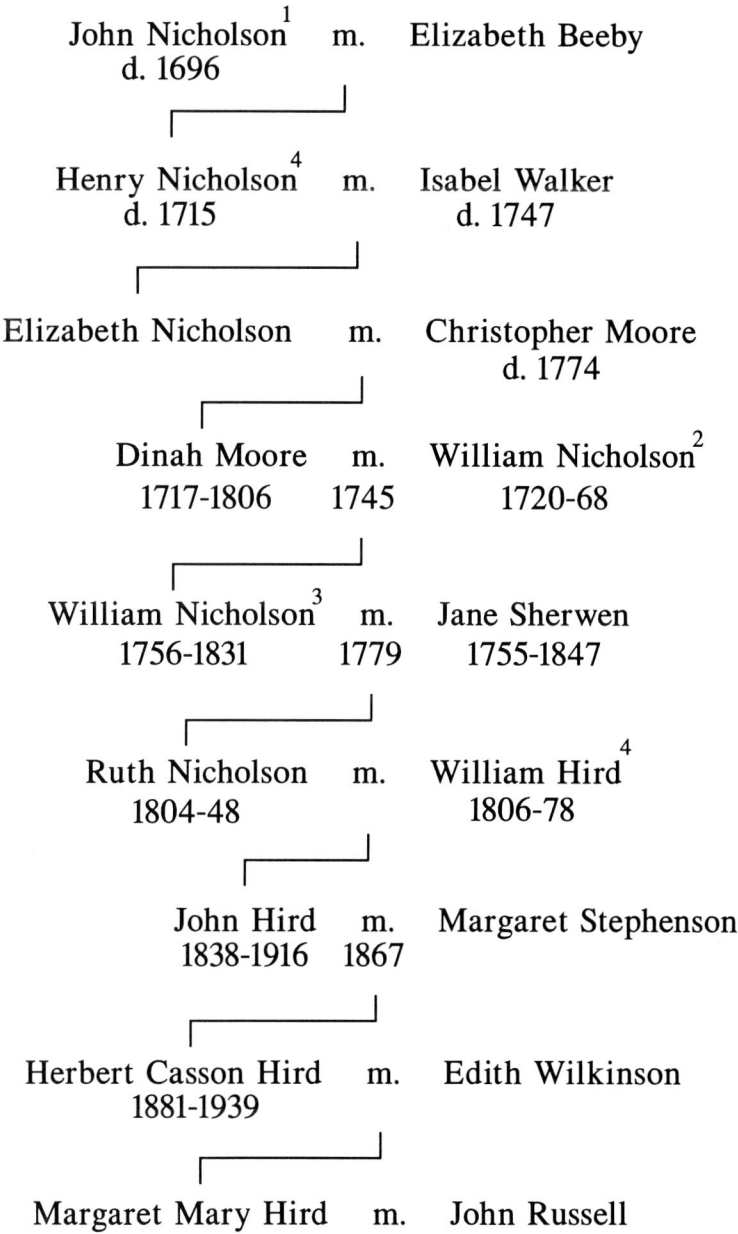

John Nicholson[1]   m.   Elizabeth Beeby
d. 1696

Henry Nicholson[4]   m.   Isabel Walker
d. 1715   d. 1747

Elizabeth Nicholson   m.   Christopher Moore
                                          d. 1774

Dinah Moore   m.   William Nicholson[2]
1717-1806   1745   1720-68

William Nicholson[3]   m.   Jane Sherwen
1756-1831   1779   1755-1847

Ruth Nicholson   m.   William Hird[4]
1804-48   1806-78

John Hird   m.   Margaret Stephenson
1838-1916   1867

Herbert Casson Hird   m.   Edith Wilkinson
1881-1939

Margaret Mary Hird   m.   John Russell

NICHOLSON ANCESTORS
(Randlehow & Yatthouse)

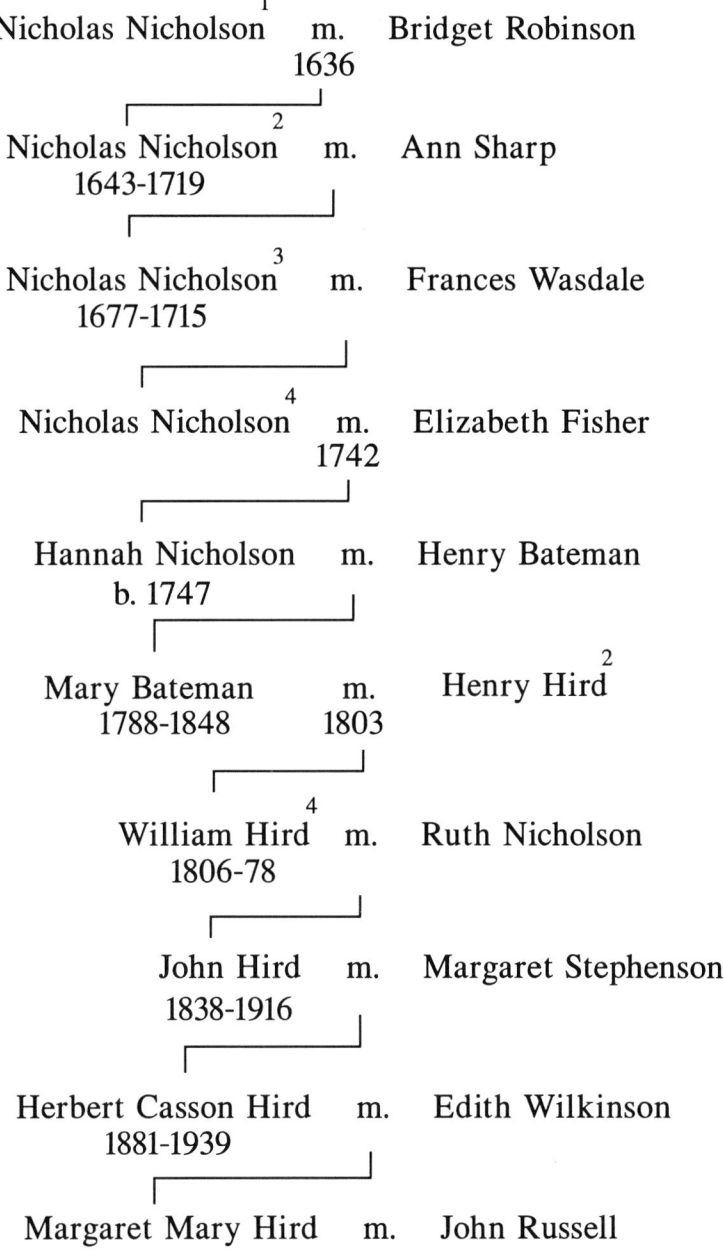

Nicholas Nicholson[1]   m.   Bridget Robinson
                   1636

Nicholas Nicholson[2]   m.   Ann Sharp
    1643-1719

Nicholas Nicholson[3]   m.   Frances Wasdale
    1677-1715

Nicholas Nicholson[4]   m.   Elizabeth Fisher
                   1742

Hannah Nicholson   m.   Henry Bateman
    b. 1747

Mary Bateman   m.   Henry Hird[2]
    1788-1848   1803

William Hird[4]   m.   Ruth Nicholson
    1806-78

John Hird   m.   Margaret Stephenson
    1838-1916

Herbert Casson Hird   m.   Edith Wilkinson
    1881-1939

Margaret Mary Hird   m.   John Russell

NICHOLSON ANCESTORS
(Bridge End, Boot)

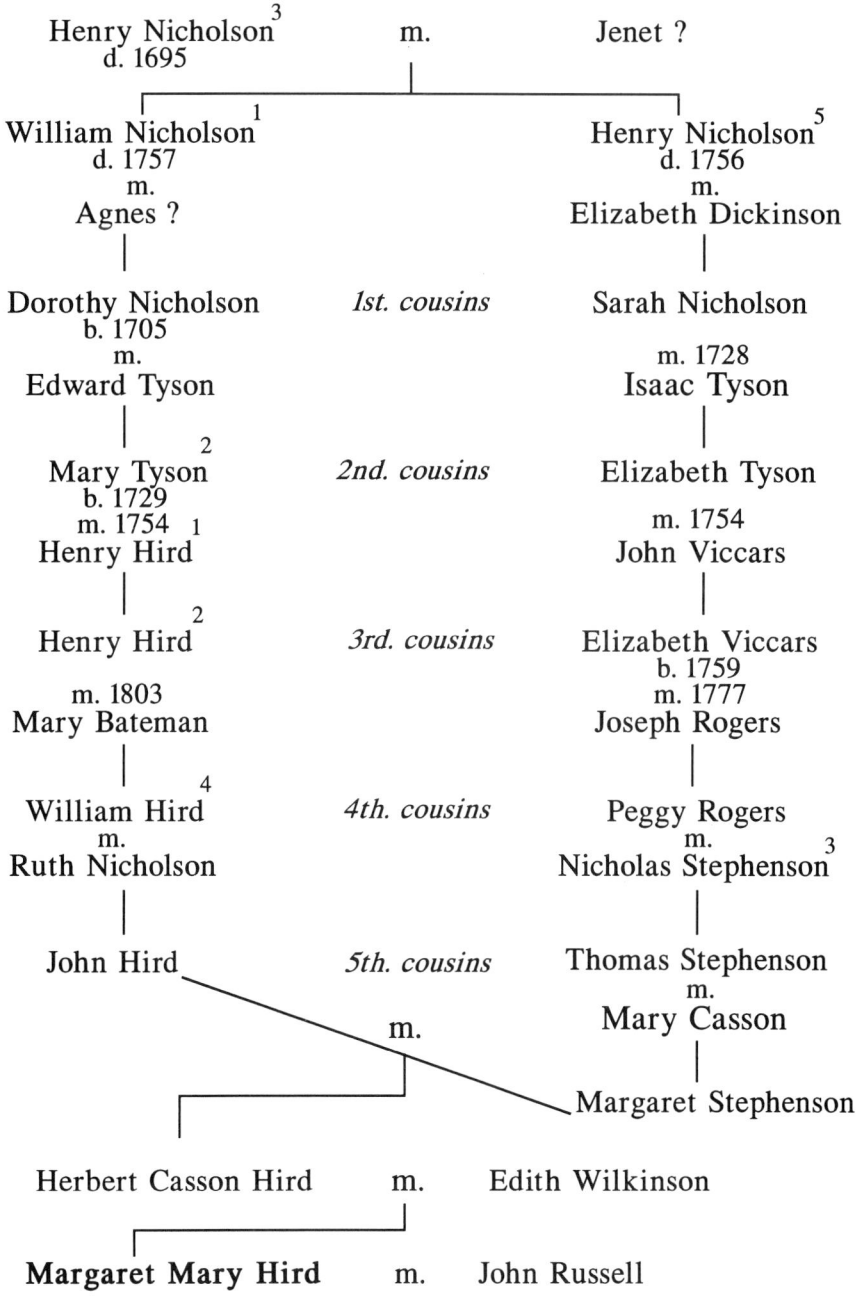

Henry Nicholson[3]   m.   Jenet ?
d. 1695

William Nicholson[1]   Henry Nicholson[5]
d. 1757   d. 1756
m.   m.
Agnes ?   Elizabeth Dickinson

Dorothy Nicholson   *1st. cousins*   Sarah Nicholson
b. 1705
m.   m. 1728
Edward Tyson   Isaac Tyson

Mary Tyson[2]   *2nd. cousins*   Elizabeth Tyson
b. 1729
m. 1754 [1]   m. 1754
Henry Hird   John Viccars

Henry Hird[2]   *3rd. cousins*   Elizabeth Viccars
                                         b. 1759
m. 1803   m. 1777
Mary Bateman   Joseph Rogers

William Hird[4]   *4th. cousins*   Peggy Rogers
m.   m.
Ruth Nicholson   Nicholas Stephenson[3]

John Hird   *5th. cousins*   Thomas Stephenson
                                             m.
                    m.   Mary Casson

                                        Margaret Stephenson

Herbert Casson Hird   m.   Edith Wilkinson

Margaret Mary Hird   m.   John Russell

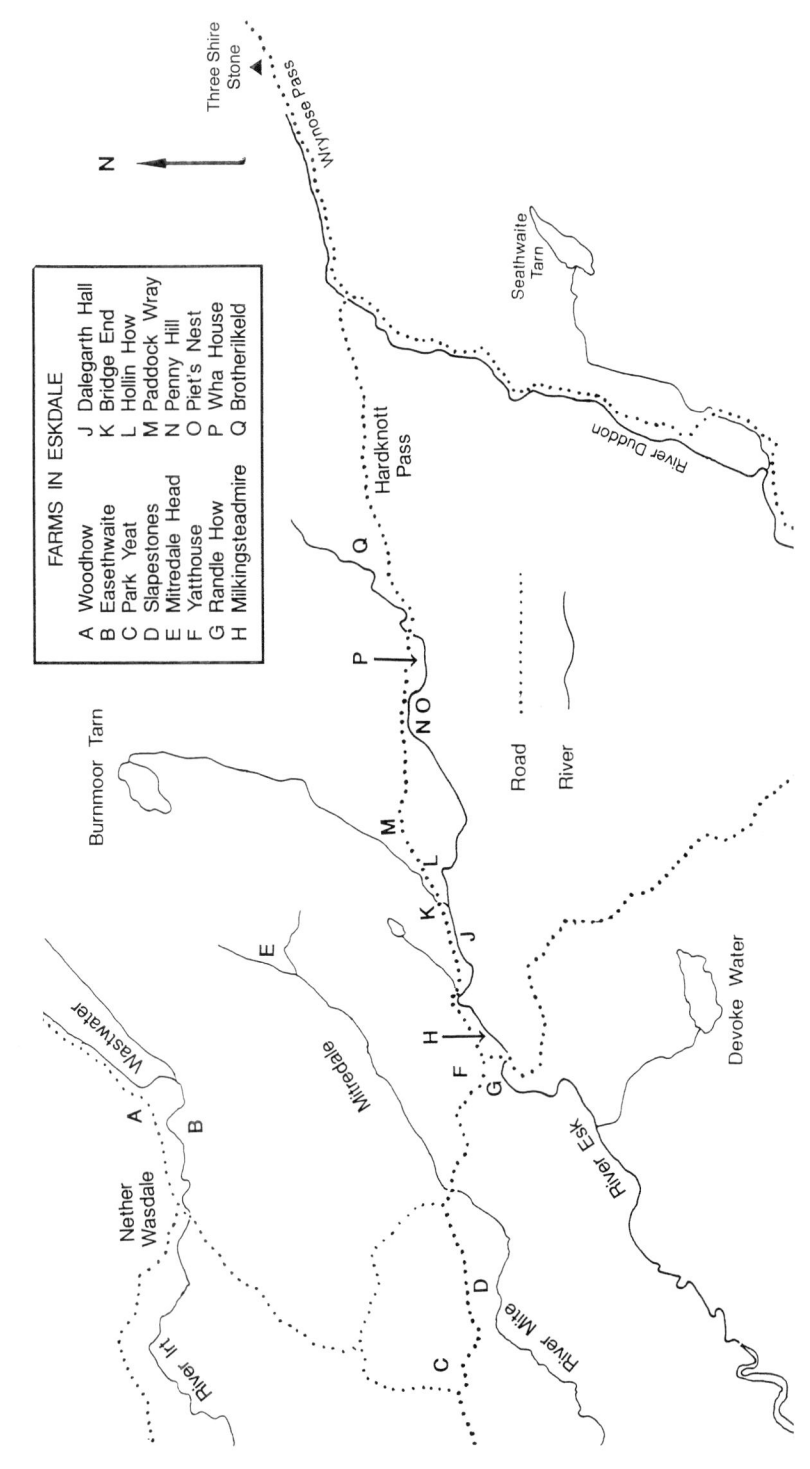

FARMS IN ESKDALE

A Woodhow	J Dalegarth Hall
B Easethwaite	K Bridge End
C Park Yeat	L Hollin How
D Slapestones	M Paddock Wray
E Mitredale Head	N Penny Hill
F Yatthouse	O Piet's Nest
G Randle How	P Wha House
H Milkingsteadmire	Q Brotherilkeld

Road ....

River

N

Three Shire Stone

Wrynose Pass

Seathwaite Tarn

River Duddon

Hardknott Pass

Burnmoor Tarn

Wastwater

Nether Wasdale

River Irt

Mitredale

River Mite

River Esk

Devoke Water

PART 3 - THE NICHOLSONS

Nicholson Ancestors -
the Nicholsons of Nether Wasdale and Slapestones, Irton

'Three Miss Nicholsons rode over from Nether Wasdale to attend a dance at Ulpha, they fell in love with three local boys and married them.' This was told to me by Thomas Dawson, mentioned in the last chapter, when I was about eleven years old. It fascinated me; I knew that dances went on until around three in the morning and also that the young man with whom a lady had the last waltz was expected to take her home. Now it was a long way from Ulpha to Nether Wasdale, so how did those young men get back in time to do the milking?

Thus the seed of Family History was planted. It lay dormant during my teenage years, just throwing up a small shoot when I heard something of interest, until about forty years ago, when it began to blossom. Thomas Dawson could also remember my great, great, grandmother perishing on her way to Penny Hill and many more exciting stories. There was a headstone in Ulpha Churchyard which referred to the Hirds and Nicholsons, which I used to read when we wandered around the graves before Sunday School. We knew who everyone was that was buried in the New Churchyard and a lot in the old one, it was quite a natural thing to do in those days. Relationships were never discussed, but we certainly knew who were strangers in the valley! It was only in later life, when I began my research, that I found out that Thomas Dawson was a kinsman.

The Nicholsons were the first ancestors that I began to research, nearly forty years ago, and they are possibly my favourites. As you will read, I have several different lines, all in some way connecting with Hirds and other ancestors. Nicholson was a common name in Cumberland, especially in the western part, not so much in Westmorland and Furness. I suspect these Nicholsons were of Cumberland origin, but, having said that I realise that it is a name that appears in many parts of the country.

I think that the three sisters mentioned above and their brother, were the first to come to the Duddon Valley, with the exception of a John Nicholson a 'slategetter' who was married at Seathwaite in 1761 and had a child baptised there later the same year and earlier, a Henry Nicholson from Eskdale who took up residence in Ulpha - but more about him later.

Now for a brief history of the lads the sisters married. My great-grandmother was Ruth Nicholson, the youngest of the three sisters;

she married my great-grandfather, William Hird[4]. Her sister Ann married William Stables and the third sister, Jane, married Robert Jenkinson. Each marriage produced a number of children, so there were many cousins in the valley.

The Stables family had long been settled in the valley and had married into numerous families. There is a History of them, written by a descendant, Dr. Brian Conlong, going back into the 16c. There is still a representative of this family living in Ulpha.

The Jenkinsons are more elusive; some were living in Seathwaite and the one that Jane wed had connections with Whitehaven. A stout headstone in Ulpha churchyard gives the following;

> *In Memory of James Crosby Jenkinson of Whitehaven*
> *Who perished on Birker Moor during*
> *'the pelting of the Pitiless Storm'*
> *on 1ˢᵗ· January 1826*
> *aged 17years.*
> *Also Robert Jenkinson*
> *Father of the above*
> *who died November 5ᵗʰ· 1852*
> *aged 89 years.*

The 1851 Census gives Robert as a retired wheelsmith, born in Seathwaite, living at Holehouse, Ulpha, with two unmarried daughters, Betsy aged 50 and Agnes, 38, both born in Whitehaven.

Research has revealed that, at the time the Nicholson girls rode to that dance, they had a brother, William[4], farming in Seathwaite. Further research shows that none of the three were married in Nether Wasdale, as might be expected. They were the three youngest children of William Nicholson[3] and Jane, née Sherwen, of Woodhow in Nether Wasdale, a tenement entered in 1756 by William's father, another William, who we will meet further on in this story.

William Nicholson[3]   m   Jane Sherwen

1779

Dinah	Bellah	Hannah	William[4]	John[3]	Ann	Jane	Ruth
1779-	1781-	1784-	1786-	1793-	1793-	1796-1838	1804-48
m	m	m	m	m	m	m	m
1800	1806	1811	1815				
Jn. Miller	Jn. Wilson	Jn. Myers	Betty Tyson	Jane Porter	William Stable(s)	Robert Jenkinson	**William**[4] **Hird**

I have managed to find information on all the members of this family, some coming through members of the Cumbria FHS. Dinah, who married John Miller for instance; their daughter married a Tyson whose descendant went to work in Glasgow in the 1800's and from there, one of his descendants moved to Leicester. (what was the pull? In the previous chapter, Hartley Dawson had worked in Glasgow. I wonder if there was a lot of building going on?)

From various wills, I have discovered information about Bellah and Hannah. Another society member had information about John and we were also able to confirm that that the Esther Nicholson, living with William Hird[4] as a servant at Moorhouse in the 1851 census, was John[3]'s daughter.

Most of the descendants of Ann and Jane lived in the valley and those of the younger generation were my friends. However, I had not been able to trace one of the Jenkinson girls until her great-grandson, Dr. Tom Atkinson from California, turned up one day on my doorstep! Tom has done a lot of research on both the Atkinsons and the Pritt families, so, with a very few missing pieces, one jigsaw is almost complete.

William[3] and Jane Nicholson's large family were born over a period of twenty-five years. Jane was twenty-four when her first child was born and forty-nine when my great-grandmother, Ruth, came into the world. Despite all this child bearing, Jane lived to be ninety-three years of age, my great-grandmother dying before her.

I had difficulty finding information about Jane Sherwen. I was told, in good faith, that she was a daughter of John Sherwen and Eleanor Russell. However, I learned my first hard lesson as a family historian, 'always, check everything yourself'. Through looking at a will, I found that this John had died several years before 'my' Jane was born! I eventually got a clue from a family bible; the inscription inside read *'to Jane Nicholson from her uncle James John Johnson of St. Bees.'* As this bible was in the possession of one of the descendants of Jane Jenkinson, I realised I was on the right track. First I found James John Johnson's will; fortunately for me he died prior to his wife as her will opened up a list of nieces and nephews. Jane was thus shown to be the daughter of John Sherwen and Isabell Porter. She was baptised at Gosforth on November 22nd. 1755 and was buried at Nether Wasdale on November 27th. 1847, a few days after her ninety-third birthday.

Before going on to the history of the Sherwens, a little social history of the times.

Social History

The year Jane was born, (1755), England declared war against France which lasted until 1765.

In 1756, Minorca (today a favourite place with holiday makers), then a possession of the English, fell to the French.

In 1765, the National Debt stood at £140 million.

Events that happened during her long life included the American War of Independence, the introduction of the penny post and the development of the railways as a means of transport.

Locally, John Paul Jones had attempted to burn down Whitehaven.

The *'Cumberland Pacquet'* or Ware's *'Whitehaven Advertiser'*, made its appearance in 1774. This paper, with lots of historical, local and family information printed on its pages, would be welcomed, I should think, by most Cumbrians.

In 1777, the paper was giving shipping information for Whitehaven, Workington, Maryport and Lancaster. This included the name of the ship, the name of the master, where it had arrived from or where it was departing to and the cargoes being carried and who they were for.

Most of the shipping was coastal, but in January of that year, on the 20th., *'The 'Tyger', with Master Storey, arrived from Jamaica;'* on 21st., *'the 'Ann', with master Thompson, sailed for Bordeaux'* and, on the 22nd. *'the 'Bellona', with Master Barras, sailed from Whitehaven for Dominica.'*

At Lancaster the list of goods imported:-

'Richard Salisbury & Co. 200 barrels of flour
John Braithwaite, 163 cow hides
Robert Jepson, hogsheads of tallow,
Greenhall & Burrow, 4 hogsheads of Tallow
Elizabeth Walshman & Co., 4 hogshead of tallow
Edward & Robert Whiteside, 50 sacks flour
Edward Herbert, 50 barrels of tar.'

All these came in the 'Friendship', master James Whittaker, from Dublin.

In 1779 the paper was reporting Marriages, at Carlisle, Liverpool, and London e.g.

January 2nd. issue *'A few days ago Mr. Wm. Dowson, merchant in Liverpool son of Mr. Dowson of this town, to Miss Parkinson of Lancaster.'*

January 19th. *'Sunday F'night at Egremont Mr. John Romey, of Craige Mill, Castleton I.O.M to Miss Molly Ford of Egremont.'*

March 30th. issue *'At Workington Peane Davis a private in the Denbighshire Militia, to Mrs Routledge an accomplished widow with 10 children.'* Brave man!

Deaths were also mentioned, e.g. May 4th. *'Lately at Wigton Mr. John Smith died, he was a soldier in Queen Anne's war and had a pension upwards of 50 years.'*

In 1780 in November a list of ships missing:-
'Egmont', 70 guns, Captain Houlton;
'Endymion', 44 guns, Captain Carteral;
'Deal Castle' 24 guns, Captain Hawkins
and *'Camelot' 24 guns, Captain Johnstone*

There is always a lighter side to all histories, and the instincts of animals through years of continuous practice as can be seen from the following:-

Whitehaven 15 th July 1794. *'On Tuesday fortnight, one William Lithgow, returning from this town to Caldbeck, from whence he had driven some cattle, was taken ill on his reaching Cockermouth: the horse on which he rode went to the door of the George Inn; the poor man was taken in: he was a native of Scotland.'* I wonder did 'a Wee Nip' bring him round!

The Sherwens

The Sherwens of Gosforth are a very old family. There is mention in 1332 of John and Richard Scherwynd paying subsidy. There are families of that name mentioned in Workington, Whitehaven, Egremont, Eskdale, Irton and Nether Wasdale, as well as Gosforth.

The earliest baptism in the Gosforth registers is July 3rd. 1573, of *'Thomas son of Robert Sherwen.'*

The earliest Copeland Will is that of Christopher of Irton in 1623. There are also two P.C.C. Wills, one of John, yeoman, of Irton 1658, who mentions his sister Margaret Kirkbride and his brother-in-law, Thomas Moor's children; the other, dated 1660, is that of John, chapman, of Gosforth Gate who must have been a most thoughtful man as his will begins,

'To every Poor widow in our parish twelve pence. Twenty shillings to be divided between the rest of the poor at my byrial' (sic)
He mentions sons, John and William and cousin Richard Copley.

Mr John Sherwen of Gosforth uttered his Nuncupative Will on the 10th. August 1701, before Mr. Thomas Kirby of Ravenglass, William Gaitskell of Bell-hill, in the parish of Drigg, Thomas Marshall and John Hartley of Lowlingbank, both in Gosforth. It was very short; he gave the sixteenth part of the ship called *'Fortune'*, wholly to his son Edward and the rest to be equally divided between the said son, daughter Isabell and his wife Catherine. His estate was valued at £214.5.2d and the inventory included *'in Gold and money £74, Bookes, Desks'* and the usual items of a yeoman, but also leather, a commodity not usually mentioned. Obviously a man of some standing as shown both by his wealth and the title 'Mister' written on the will.

A much later will which is of interest, is that of Robert Sherwen of Whitehaven, which was proved on 3rd. September 1857. He is described as *'a gentleman'*. He left to Jeremiah Tinnion, of Tallentire, One Hundred Pounds and the eight-day clock, formerly the property of his late wife, and another bequest of property belonging to his late wife to Mary Scott. He mentions his cousin, Jane Lacklinson, wife of Alexander of Scargill, St Bees. His house and premises in Plumbland Lane, Tarn Head and Brigg Dyke, Sellafield, are left in trust, to pay his nieces Elizabeth and Eleanor Sherwen forty pounds a year. The residue went to nephew John Sherwen, not heard of for a long time. A search must have been made, as notification of his death was received four years later :-

'I certify that John Sherwen was admitted into the Institution from the Ship 'Duke of Bronte' and that he died on the 6ᵗʰ April 1846 having been in Hospital 54 days from the date of his admittance 12ᵗʰ February 1846.' signed *'H.Bickersleth M.D. F.R.C.S. England Surgeon to the hospital. Somerset Hospital, Capetown, 25ᵗʰ January 1861.'*

How many sailors lie in foreign lands, many in places unknown to their kith and kin? Would John's place of death have been known had he not been mentioned in a will?

My own line of this family is from Seascale How, Gosforth.

I have already mentioned the family of Jane, who married Willian Nicholson. Her brothers and sisters also had quite large families.

John and Sarah (Sharpe) had six children, John, Peter, Samuel, William, Isabel and Sarah.
Of these, John was killed by a cart while collecting seaweed (Cororoner's Inquests CRO Carlisle).
Samuel, baptised in 1790, entered the Church and was Rector of Dean for 45 years. He married first Hannah Robinson and secondly, in Scotland, Anne Eliza Gray, but did not have family by either. (see page 173.)

Hannah married John James Johnson but had no children.

Elizabeth married Isaac Coalbank and bore three children, Hannah, Sarah and Elizabeth, who are mentioned in their Aunt Hannah's will. I think there were some more who are not mentioned. The Coalbanks were a Nether Wasdale family.

Bellah married John Huddard and of her children mentioned in the will are John, Peter, Jane, and Hannah.

Sarah married a man called Walker and Hannah's will mentions John, Edward, Isabel and Mary Walker.

Finally, the children of Peter Sherwen mentioned in this will are John, Peter, Elizabeth Ann and Eleanor.

I feel sure that there were some nephews and nieces omitted, but even with those mentioned there are about thirty first cousins. Did they all keep in touch?

I must now give a little information on Isabell Porter, as the female lines are just as important.

Gosforth Church

Porters

The Porters had been in the county for many centuries. There is reference to Henry Porter in the Calendar of Close Rolls, 1338 as having
two burgages in Egremont.

There was a family well established in the 16c. at Weary Hall in
the parish of Bolton, near Carlisle and from this family the Porters of
Low Holme and the ones of Easthwaite in Irton are descended, my
ancestors from the latter.

An extensive pedigree was published in the CWAA Vol 14 NS, by
the late Dr. C. A. Parker. In this he gives the grandparents of Isabella
as Lancelot Porter and his wife Margaret, née Cat4ericke, who seems
to have come from Yorkshire; they were Catholics. He quotes Margaret's Will, but there is no mention of any children of her own. He
goes on to say that Lancelot, who died in 1673 had his Will proved,
but it is missing. I found this Will and again there is no mention of
children. The late C. Roy Hudleston agreed with me that they were
childless, but, unfortunately, Roy died before he could publish an
amendment and before I found more information amongst the Leaconfield Papers. These show the admission, in 1699, of Isabelle's
father, Lancelot, to Usthwaite, (Easthwaite) on the death of his father,
Thomas. An earlier document, dated 1695, gives the rights and the
routes for driving sheep to the common land for Thomas Porter's
Messuage and Tenement at Easthwaite (Usthwaite).

One problem is solved, but another arises. Whose son was Thomas? So far I have not found a will to identify him. He had three
children, Lancelot, Philip and Mary.

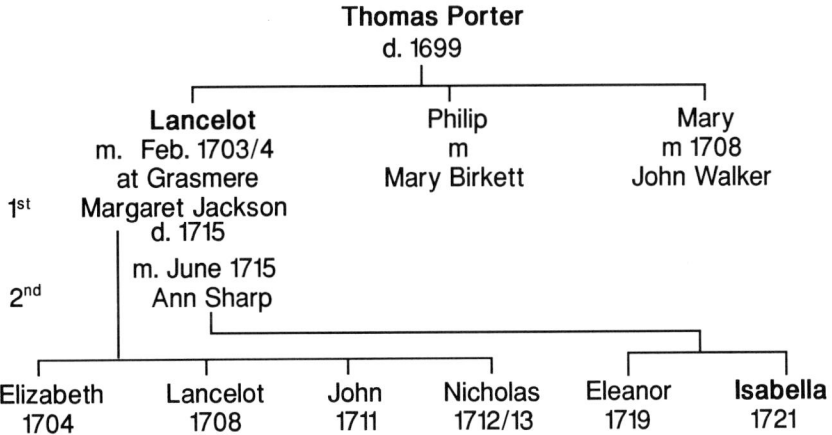

Lancelot was married at Grasmere in February 1703/4, to Margaret Jackson. She died in 1715 and was buried on the 29th. April. Lancelot remarried on the 8th. June, by Licence. His bride was Ann Sharp, spinster, and by her he had Eleanor in 1719 and 'my' Isabella who was baptised in 1721. He died in 1722 and left a will.

Philip married Mary, daughter of George Birkett. For information on his sister, Mary Porter, I quote from Dr. Parker *'John Walker of Santon, yeoman, in 1708, settled £40 on 'Mary sister of Lancelot Porter' and married her at St. Bees on June 3rd. of the same year.'* The marriage is recorded in the Irton registers. In her will of 1764, she mentions the children of both her brothers and, fortunately for me, refers to Isabella as Sherwen.

I have not been able to find the marriage of John Sherwen and Isabella Porter, but I found a Marriage Bond that gave her name as Elizabeth, (which is interchangeable with Isabelle), and as Isabelle Sherwen she was buried.

ARMS OF GEORGE PORTER
OF WEARY HALL

More Nicholsons

Sorting out the families is no easy task when so many have the same name. I try to cross check on each member and William Nicholson[2] father of William[3] (1756-1831) who came to Woodhow in 1756 was no exception. He married Dinah Moor and, as well as William, had Matilda in 1747, John in 1749 and Isaac in 1761. The memorials of most of them are to be found in Nether Wasdale churchyard.

From the tree below you will note the youngest son was Isaac, he became involved in the Lady Huntington Connection and was, in later life, a leading light at her College.

Son John's son John, became a merchant in London, retiring to Dorking where he died in 1850. His daughter left money to build Ulpha Vicarage and money in a trust to aid young men of the area towards their education to enable them to enter the Church. No further information can be found about the Trust. The vicarage is now in private hands.

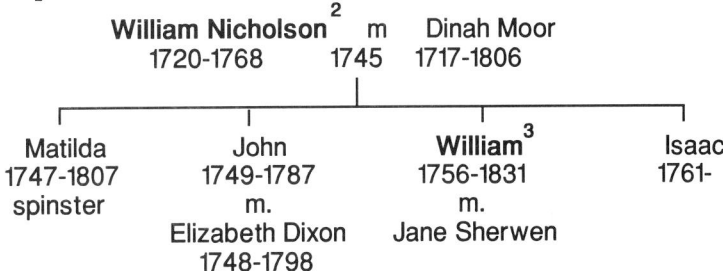

Two more children, Christopher and Ruth died in infancy.

But who *was* William[2]?. I had been given a tree that said he was a descendant of John of Slapestones, but I was not happy with it, so once again, with aid of wills and Manorial Records I am going to try to show why.

The descendants of John Nicholson of Slapestones, who died in 1694, are another example of family connections. Dinah Moor was a descendant of this family.

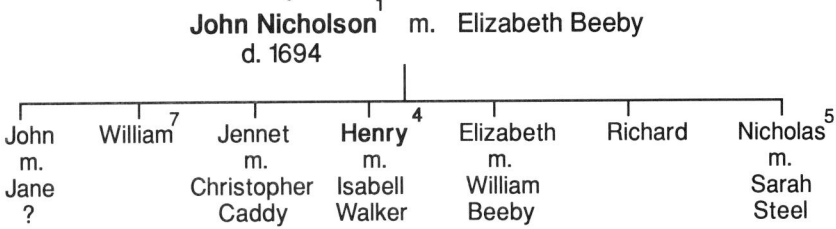

I met Ruth Geldart, of Clive, near Shrewsbury, in the 1970s; she was a descendant of Nicholas Nicholson[5] and Sarah Steele. We pooled our resources, Ruth having much more information than I had, for she had already been researching for thirty years! When the Cumbria Family History Society was founded, she was the first editor of the Newsletter and continued until her death in 1984. Ruth was convinced that I too, was descended from Nicholas[5] as well as from Henry[4] and Isobell Walker. Family histories take years of research and patience to complete; the task is even greater when there are so many of the same name in the same places.

Fortunately, both John[1], who died in 1694 and his wife, Elizabeth, left good wills, both referring to a grandchild, Isaac Nicholson, and neither to a son of that name. Yet the Rev. C. Moor, in his *'Erminois'* (more of him later), states that there was a son Isaac; this, however, is not true. He also speaks of the possibility that there was another daughter, who married a Powle. This could well be true, even though John makes no mention in his will, Elizabeth refers to her granddaughters Ann and Jennet Powle.

One interesting clause in John[1]'s will is that he leaves £5 each to his sons William[7] and Richard in full satisfaction of their part and portion stating *'And it is my Will and Mind that my two said sons William and Richard shall come themselves to receive their legacies herin by me given them, And give my Executors a Sufficient discharge for the same, or otherwise the said legacies shall fall and be redeemed to my Estate.'* I wonder where they had gone? Possibly to war, or migrated to another part of the country. Will we ever know?

John[1] also left unto James Braithwaite and his three youngest children five shillings. Who this James was I do not know, but an administration bond of Jane Braithwaite, 1705, had the following attached:

'Thomas Brockbank These are to Certify you or any other That Jane Brathwt. of Irton, when she deceased Left Noo Estate, But only Four Pounds in Disperat Debt Soo her Father being A poore Man, was forced to Borrow Money to Burie her with, And her Father being one of the poore of this pish this is all which your Friend and Sryt. knowes.
John Nicholson [4] Randlehow January 22nd. 1705'

Another John Nicholson, from another family, we shall hear more of him later.

Elizabeth Nicholson died in1699, five years after her husband and bequeathed

'... unto my sonne John, Twenty Shillings in full part for his part forth of my Estate:
Item: I give unto his son Isaac ten shillings:
Item I give to my sonne John Nicholson sonne John Nicholson ten shillings Upon Condition, that is to say, that if my sonne John Nicholson and his sonne John doo promise suffer law & Liberty unto my sonne Henry Nicholson to goo and come through their ground at Slaestone when he hath occacasion to goo and use to and from Morthwaite During his Natural life.'

I wonder if that right of way exists today, three hundred years later.

Elizabeth's personal estate disposal gives an insight to what clothes ladies wore three hundred years ago: to her grandchild Ann Powle *'my Red Coat*, to her daughter, Jane Caddy *'my best coat and waistcoat'* and then all her *'Linning Apparrell'* was to be equally divided between her five daughters, with no distinction between natural daughters and daughters-in-law. *'William Beebey Wife, Christopher Caddy Wife, John Nicholson wife, Nicholas Nicholson Wife and Henry Nicholson Wife.'* Her Trunk (did she travel or keep her clothes in it?) was left to son John's daughter Sarah and to John she left one feather bed with the furniture belonging.

Henry Nicholson[4] of Parkyeat, in Irton, tanner, the third son of John[1] and Elizabeth is my direct ancestor, so I will begin with him. He married Isabel daughter of Richard and Elizabeth Walker of Sandbank in Irton. He died 1715 and is buried at Irton

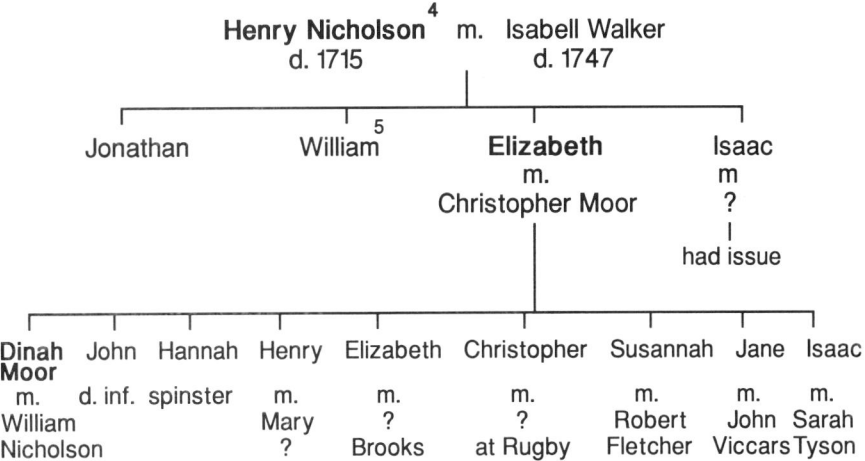

Henry[4], in his will proved on 27[th.] September 1715, expressed doubt whether his second son William[5] would be pronounced heir to his two estates, and charged him, in that case, to give £30, *'which my son Jonathan was obliged to give'* to his younger children, Elizabeth and Isaac. Was he living away or perhaps in the army?

Isabell Nicholson his widow, also buried at Irton, 10[th.] December 1747, by her will, proved 13[th.] May 1748, left one shilling to her eldest son Jonathan for his filial portion, *'if he come to demand it,'* and she also had doubts whether William[5] would *'come and enjoy'* the parcells of ground, one in Irton called Parkyeat the other in Muncaster called Murthat. What had become of these two sons? So many unsolved mysteries.

Before we deal with the descendants of Nicholas[5] we must consider the Moors.

The Moor(e) Family

The Moore family had long been associated with Irton. The books and papers of the Rev. Dr. C. Moor helped me a great deal with this line. Researchers in this area owe him a lot. His books *'Erminois'*, and *'The Fletcher Case'*, together with his papers in the C & W AA, have helped me tremendously.

In *'Erminois'*, he traces his descent from Nicholas Moor or Moore of Cragg, who died before 1583/4. From this pedigree, in 1816, Arms were granted:

> Erminois on a chevron engrailed Sable between
> Three moorcocks Proper a mitre between two
> Crosses pattee Or.
> Crest A Moor's arm embowed Proper the hand
> Grasping two javelins towards the dexter broken Or

In 1917, the above mentioned Rev. Dr. Moor was granted a Badge to perpetuate the memory of his eldest son, Lieut. Christopher Moor, B.A. (Cantab.), the Hampshire Regiment, (1892-1915), who was killed in action at Gallipolli.

> The Badge, A crux absata (or ankh) Or.

(the ankh is the ancient Egyption sign of Life, not before used in English heraldry)
Ref. Cumb. Families & Heraldry, Hudleston & Boumphry)

Nicholas Moor of Irton was my 10th great grandfather. I think the direct line of descent worthy of inclusion in this book.

[Please see the next page]

I have checked all the wills and administration bonds for the Moors, but the marriages of John Moor of Cragg (d. 1704/5) are taken from *'Erminois'*. There is a similarity in some of these wills to that of John Nicholson of Randlehow, in the possession of books and other items to be kept as heirlooms.

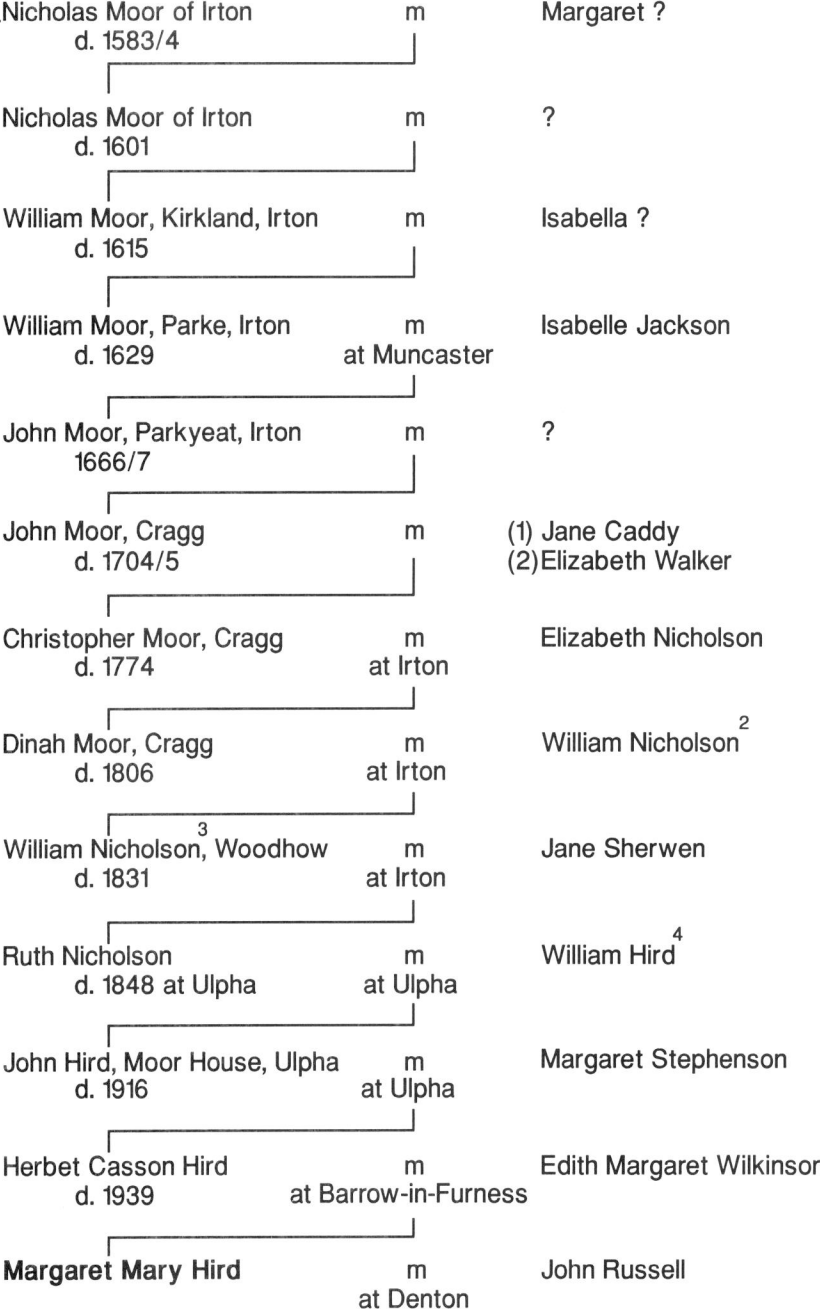

.Nicholas Moor of Irton d. 1583/4	m	Margaret ?
Nicholas Moor of Irton d. 1601	m	?
William Moor, Kirkland, Irton d. 1615	m	Isabella ?
William Moor, Parke, Irton d. 1629	m at Muncaster	Isabelle Jackson
John Moor, Parkyeat, Irton 1666/7	m	?
John Moor, Cragg d. 1704/5	m	(1) Jane Caddy (2)Elizabeth Walker
Christopher Moor, Cragg d. 1774	m at Irton	Elizabeth Nicholson
Dinah Moor, Cragg d. 1806	m at Irton	William Nicholson[2]
William Nicholson[3], Woodhow d. 1831	m at Irton	Jane Sherwen
Ruth Nicholson d. 1848 at Ulpha	m at Ulpha	William Hird[4]
John Hird, Moor House, Ulpha d. 1916	m at Ulpha	Margaret Stephenson
Herbet Casson Hird d. 1939	m at Barrow-in-Furness	Edith Margaret Wilkinson
Margaret Mary Hird	m at Denton	John Russell

This pedigree covers thirteen generations in four hundred years.

John Moore of Parkyeat, (d. 1666/7), when referring to his son John, couples his name with Elizabeth Mawson, this, the Rev. Dr. Moor thought, might be that he had recently married Elizabeth and that he was adhering to the old Scottish custom of referring to a wife by her maiden name. Maybe so, but I'm inclined to think that there were, three hundred years ago, what today are known as 'partners' or 'common-law wives'.

John Moor of Cragg, who died 1704/5, appointed John Nicholson of Randlehow, one of the feoffees, to see his will performed. He must have had an extensive library, as he left one third of his books, together with his silver seal, to a grandson, Christopher; another third, together with his Bible, to son Christopher, and the final third to be divided between his son-in-law John Hodgkin's son John, and the children of his daughter-in-law, Widow Moore. This widow is Christopher's mother who on February 2[nd.] 1705/6 was married at St. Bees, to John Walker of Sandbank; she subsequently produced more children.

Before returning to the descendants of Nicholas Nicholson[5], I will just mention the family of Christopher Moor and Elizabeth Nicholson. They had nine children. (see tree on p.101)

Henry, the eldest surviving son, inherited Cragg; he had four children:
Elizabeth (b. 1755) who married Henry Casson of Drigg. They had two daughters.
Susan (b. 1757) married Michael Dawson of Grasmere. They had four sons baptised at Ambleside.
Christopher (b.1760) inherited Cragg.
Mary (b. 1764) married John Rigg of Windermere and had one daughter.
(More examples of Cumberland/Westmorland marriages.)

Christopher, the next son, entered the church and was of Rugby.

Isaac Moor, the youngest son, was a shopkeeper at Ravenglass. He married Sarah Tyson of Penny Hill, Birker who was a descendant of William Stephenson and Margaret Gibson, of Crosbythwaite.

Dinah, the eldest daughter, my ancestor, as you have seen, married William Nicholson[2].

Hannah remained a spinster.

Elizabeth married a man called Brooks.

Susannah married Robert Fletcher of Wasdale, whose descendant, Christopher, left an interesting will leaving money to his cousins. A court case was needed to decide who were cousins and who were second cousins. Many, many families were eligible for a share and, as I said earlier, the Rev. Dr. Moor compiled a book relating to the case. This was published privately and I am fortunate to have a copy.

Jane, the youngest daughter, married John Viccars of Eskdale. Their descendants today are scattered far and wide.

Nether Wasdale Church

Nicholas Nicholson of Slapestones

Nicholas Nicholson[5], youngest son of John[1] of Slapestones (see page 99) married Sarah, daughter of Edward Steele of Slapethwaite. I think they had six children.

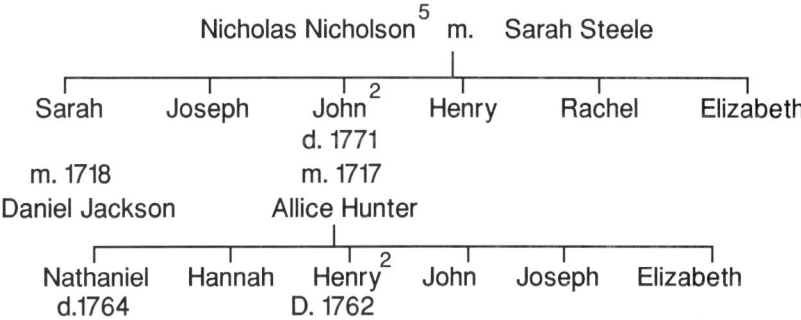

Ruth Geldert, who researched this family, thought that the William Nicholson[2] who married Dinah Moore was a son of this John and Allice, but I can find neither a baptism nor any mention in wills.

In 1762, Henry[2] died; he was a tanner of Burnbouth. In his will he gave and bequeathed to his loving wife Elizabeth all his goods, quick and dead and money and stock in trade, provided she be free and willing to let his father, John Nicholson[2], have the Bowerhouse Estate as *'I had it from him'*. The witnesses to this will were John Hartley and Jon Askew. There is no mention of a brother William, and no inventory survives.

In 1771, John Nicholson[2] of Egremont, yeoman, made his will, which is quite interesting. To his loving wife Allice he left, *'one five Guinea piece of Gould* (sic) *two large silver spoons and all my plate.'* (for once not as heirlooms)

To son Joseph, *'the Iron Weight Beam, all the weights and all the Utensils and the pan and press hammers Knives the Iron Sive* (sic) *with all movable things Belonging to the Tanyard at Burnbouth. Also the writing desk at Egremont, the wainscot chest, three cubards* (sic) *at Bowerhouse, the log table and the frames & forms, also all the graits* (sic) *and Crooks at Bowerhouse.'* Not a bad haul!

To grandson John Nicholson[7] (I presume the son of Nathaniel, who died in 1764) the *'Tanyard at Egremont with all my rights there'*, on condition he pays money, to Hannah Mawson, his aunt, and to William Holmes and William Braithwaite, who John described as his sons-in-law, so there must have been three daughters. Still no mention of a son William, a daughter-in-law or grandchildren.

Likewise, in her will, Allice, who died shortly after her husband, made no mention of a son, William. She left the Five Guinea Piece to her son-in-law, William Braithwaite, together with a plaid Quilt, a Side Saddle and a pewter dish.

I cannot believe that if John[2] and Allice had had a son William, he or his children would be omitted from both wills. My opinion was strengthened, when I found, among the D/Lec Manorial Papers, the admittance of a William Nicholson of Scarbrough (Scar Brow) in the parish of Gosforth County of Cumberland on 9[th.] June 1756, to two tenements which were at Woodhow; and *'Dinah, his wife'* admitted to another, close by, called Brown How.

Over the years, various members of William's kin held mortgages and from these deeds I have sorted out many of the descendants. Throughout my researches I have felt that the William Nicholson[2] who married Dinah Moor, was a Nicholson from Scar Brow, Gosforth. However, I have yet to prove it.

Slapestones

Nicholsons of Randlehow and Yatthouse, Eskdale.

Randlehow

That all the Nicholsons in the immediate area, Irton, Eskdale, and Boot are related, I have not yet been able to prove, maybe I shall never manage it, but one keeps trying. No one *completes* a family tree! I suspect that John[1] of Slapestones (d. 1694) and Nicholas[1] of Randlehow, (see below), were brothers. The earliest information I have on this last line is the marriage of Nicholas Nicholson[1] and Bridget Robinson at Eskdale in 1636. They were my sixth great-grandparents.

Bridget was a widow by 1655/6 when John[4] (b. 1639) and still an infant, was admitted tenant by Bridget his mother and guardian, to Randlehow of a yearly rent of two shilings and three pence. (D/Lec/311) When and where Nicholas[1] had died I have not discovered, he was alive in 1648, when he was taken before the jury by Nicholas Dickinson over pasture ground (D/Lec/265/237) so his death was obviously between then and 1655. These were troubled times - had he been called to fight?

See tree on the next page, from which descendants are spread all over the world. many trying to trace their roots.

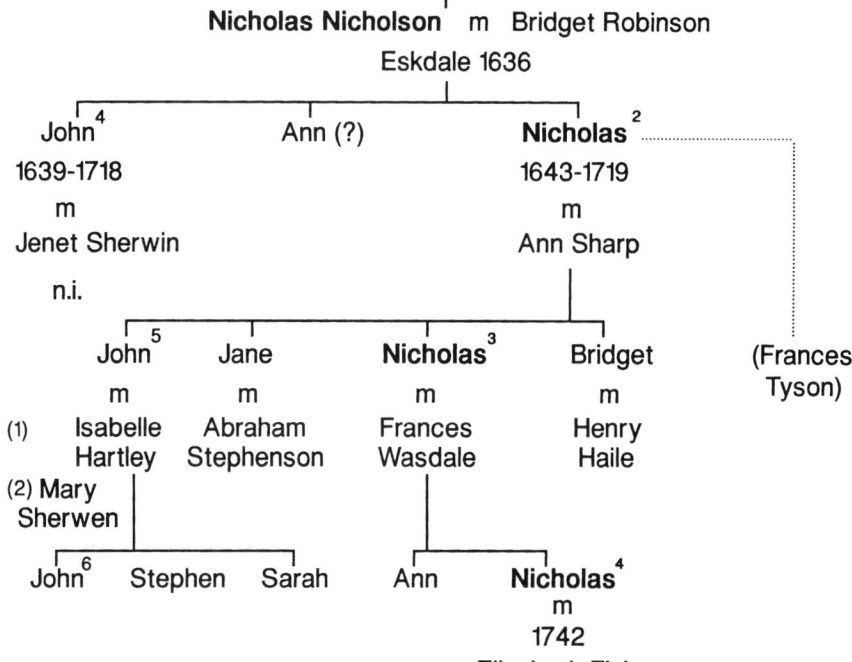

Nicholas Nicholson[1] m Bridget Robinson
Eskdale 1636

John[4] 1639-1718 m Jenet Sherwin n.i.

Ann (?)

Nicholas[2] 1643-1719 m Ann Sharp

(Frances Tyson)

John[5] m (1) Isabelle Hartley (2) Mary Sherwen

Jane m Abraham Stephenson

Nicholas[3] m Frances Wasdale

Bridget m Henry Haile

John[6]   Stephen   Sarah

Ann   Nicholas[4] m 1742 Elizabeth Fisher

Yatthouse

Social History

In 1633, after Charles I. had ruled for nine years without a parliament, Laud became Primate, reforming the Church and in particular advocating utmost leniency towards Catholics. Wentworth became Lord Deputy in Ireland, doing a good job, pursuing the suppressing of piracy, disciplining the army and developing commerce and industry.

1634 saw the revival of 'ship-money', taxation of the maritime counties to support the fleet.

By 1642, Civil war had broken out and in 1649 the United Kingdom had become a Commonwealth, continuing so until 1660. During this period, in 1655, war broke out with Spain and an English squadron captured Jamaica, thus giving the British a foothold in the West Indies.

In 1660, The Coldstream Guards were retained as the nucleus of a standing army then, in 1661, the first of a series of persecuting statutes were passed against Dissenters. By 1663, maybe earlier, these were being enforced in many parts of Cumberland and Westmorland. e. g.:-

In that year seizures were made on James Stainton of Wasdale to the value of £27 and upwards, for a demand of about £3 for Tithes.

In 1677, John Graham of Rockcliffe was presented for *'not appearing at Church to take the Oath and office of Church Warden'.*

At Skaleby, at the same court, Roland James, John Richardson, John and Richard Goodfellow and John Pearson were presented 'Ifor not paying their Assessments for mending the Church Door and hanging the Bells.'

At All Hallows, in 1669, Francis Salkeld and Annas his wife, were brought before the Church Courts for *'not coming to take communion and Robert Ritson for not paying Church Assessments.'*

Despite such prosecutions, normal events were still taking place. e.g. in 1667 there is an Apprenticeship Record (WDX/66 Kendal RO) showing Peter Kellet son of Robert Kellet of Witherslack to his father Robert Kellett, linnen webster, for seven years.

In 1678, a *'List of all the Seamen, Boatmen or Fishermen within the County of Cumberland between the ages of 18 and 50 years'* was taken. It lists them in two categories, married and unmarried.

Belonging to Whitehaven there were listed:-
62 unmarried living in the town, with Mungo Wykcliffe of Sanwith, Wm. Smith of St. Bees and Wm. Benn of Hensingham.
There were 32 married, James Ben & Rich. Kessick being of Hensingham & Wm. Woodhall of Lowcay.

Belonging to Workington 12 unmarried and 13 married. Of the latter, John Kay & Chr. Knott were of Harrington, John Thompson of Seaton, Peter Fearon of Distington, John Phillipson of Winscale, John Dale of Deane & Rich Lowes & John Thompson both of Lowcay.

Married boatmen and fishermen in Muncaster are listed as 4 from Ravenglass, 2 from Drigg and John Smith from Mitebank. Unmarried are 5, one from Ravenglass the others from Drigg.

Holme Cultrum lists 6 married, and 9 unmarried.

Allanby, one Nicho. Beeby.

Crosscanonby, 3 married and 4 unmarried.

Flimby lists 5 Married and 6 Unmarried

and Dearham gives 3 of each status.

John Nicholson[4] of Randlehow, Blacksmith.

During his long life, through the reign of five monarchs and the Commonwealth Period and into the reign of George I, John[4] must have witnessed many changes. He was a well educated man, as can be seen from his signature and mention of him in a large proportion of the wills of the inhabitants of Eskdale, Irton and Wasdale as an executor, appraisor, trustee, or supervisor. One wonders how he had time to work.

There is a lintel over the door at Randlehow, carved with the date, 1679, his initials, J.N and the tools of his trade. He would be about forty years of age when this was done; was that when he married Jenet Sherwen?

John's smithy must have been busy. An account survives from the new blast furnace at Backbarrow showing that, in the year 1713, he spent £18.5.2d on iron. That furnace had opened only in 1711.

John[4] died in January, 1718 and his will, made in 1717 was proved on February 18[th.] 1718. Parts of it are worthy of inclusion here.

*'In the name of God Amen, I John Nicholson .... I give and bequeath unto my wife Jenett Nicholson Forty-three pounds, Forty-three shillings to be paid within two months after my decease and the remainder thereof to be paid at the year's end, with the use of my Best Feather Bed & Bolster, two pair of the Best Sheets & Two pair of the second Two Pair of Blankets Two Covercloths and pillow and the best Bedspread during her life. The Bedstead not to be Removed but to remain as an **heirloom**, in full for her share ...... And in lue of her Widow bed with thirty shillings more yearly to be paid her or her*

assigns by my executor yearly and every year during her natural Life upon condition that she shall take the rent of Thirty Shillings of him or his assigns for her share & widow part of the Messuage & Tenement of Randlehow yearly during her natural life.'

To his brother Nicholas[2], (my direct ancestor) he left *'Three Pounds to be paid in six yearly instalments of ten shillings,'* adding *'if he lives so long'* (!)

To his nephew, John Nicholson[5], he bequeathed *'Thirteen Pounds which I have lying upon John Myre of Whitbeck freeland, Whether it comes in money or land:*
Item: I give and bequeath unto My Late Nephew Nicholas's daughter Ann Four Pounds' (Nicholas[3] predeceased his father) *'to be paid into the hands of John Wasdall'* (Ann's grandfather) *'and Abraham Stephenson whom I appoint to take that the same be served for the use of the said Ann until she comes to the age of One & twenty.'* He goes on to say that if Ann does not survive to the magic age, then it was to go to her brother and should he die, back into the estate. They took no chances were money was concerned!
Back to the will
'And if it please God that my late Nephew Nicholas's son, Nicholas [4] *live until he be admitted Tenent to a Tenement Caled Yathouse I give unto him Five Pounds to pay his fine with'*
He leaves money to various other great nephews and nieces, adding *'what Modest interest as comes between them Except so much as shall pay the School Master for their Learning'*
'Item; I give unto my said nephew John Nicholson [5] *'s son John* [6] *my Two Largest Silver Spoons but his father shall have the use of them when he pleases'*

To take care of the money he left to the two sons of nephew John[5], he appointed Abraham Stephenson and Thomas Hartley of Bough, *'to put the same forth for Moderate Interest'* and for their *'care and pains'* he gave them each five shillings
'I give to my Godson Robert Stephenson' (later Curate of Corney and Vicar of Innes) *'Five Shillings. I give to my Godson John Nicholson of Underbarrow, smith, Ten Shillings & Ten shillings more unto his son John Nicholson.'* (not yet researched)
He left twenty shillings to his cousin, Susan Smith of Halsenna and also the money *'... her husband is owing me*
Item; I give unto Frances Nicholson alias Tyson the reputed daughter of my Brother Nicholas Nicholson Three Pounds.' (She is my kinswoman and I know very little about her) *'I give to my cousin Marmaduke Lambert and his wife Five shillings to buy either of them a pair of gloves.'*

He gave *'Ten Shillings to be divided amongst the needful Poor of the Chapplery of Eskdale, ... Twenty Shillings towards building a Stone Bridge at Atkinson Ford and a Washfould there.'* The residue went to his nephew John Nicholson[5] whom he also made his executor, with John Stanley Esq. and the lawyer, William Gilpin of Whitehaven, to act as supervisors. For these two for their *'care and pains I give unto either of them A broad piece of Gold'.* (This was worth about £1. Coins were in short supply then).

I cannot place his cousins, Susan Smith and Marmaduke Lambert; I think they must be on his mother, Bridget Robinson's line.

Listed in his goods and chattels are his *'Sword & Apparell'* worth £3.15, a *'Part Gun, and A Clock'* also his part of the smithy tools, so he must already have taken his nephew John, into partnership. Research suggests that his brother, Nicholas, also had a smithy at or near Yatthouse. I like one listed item, *'An Hors'* and was delighted to see that, like me, he had a collection of *'Books to the value of £1 worth'* - the same as the 'Hors' and silver spoons! The total estate was £249.5.6d. so he was a wealthy man.

His wife, Jennet, died in 1721, making the son of Nicholas[2] her executor and asking that he gave her a decent send off. She mentions her sister Dorothy Stephenson, nieces Bridget Haile, Bridget Beeby, Rebecca Tubman and Rebecca Tubman daughter of William Tubman, but no relationships are given. Nephews Robert Stephenson, John Nicholson[5]'s two sons John[6] and Stephen and his daughter Sarah, also godson Thomas Stephenson.

Jane Nicholson,
4th great-granddaughter of
Nicholas Nicholson[1] and
Bridget Robinson,
great-granddaughter of
John Nicholson[6]

Nicholas Nicholson[2] of Yeathouse (Yatthouse)

Although not proven, I believe that Yeathouse was the ancestral home of the Nicholsons, but more of that later. Nicholas[2], my 5th. great-grandfather, was the second son of Nicholas and Bridget. Born in 1642, he died in October 1719. He was married to Ann, daughter of William Sharp of Hollinghead, who, when he died in 1685, left *'£10 to his son-in-law Nicholas Nicholson & his wife Ann.'* Ann must have predeceased her husband, Nicholas, as she is not mentioned in his will. His eldest son, Nicholas[3], also died four years before him. In his will, Nicholas[2] also acknowledges his *'supposed daughter Frances Nicholson alais Tyson'* and left her £5, asking that she give his Executor a Lawful Discharge. Who was Frances's mother? Doing family history, one usually wonders who the father was, here we have the reverse. Who did Frances marry? I would dearly love to know. Another possibility arises, did her mother come as a housekeeper after Ann had died? One good thing is, she was recognised by both her father and uncle.

Nicholas[2] was not as wealthy as his brother, his total estate being only £57.12.8d which included his smithy tools valued as follows;-

'Iron new & ould (sic), *£1.10s.,*
Anvil, Bellows, with other tools £2.10s.,
Grindstones 2s.6d'
and £4.17.8d owing to him for work done.

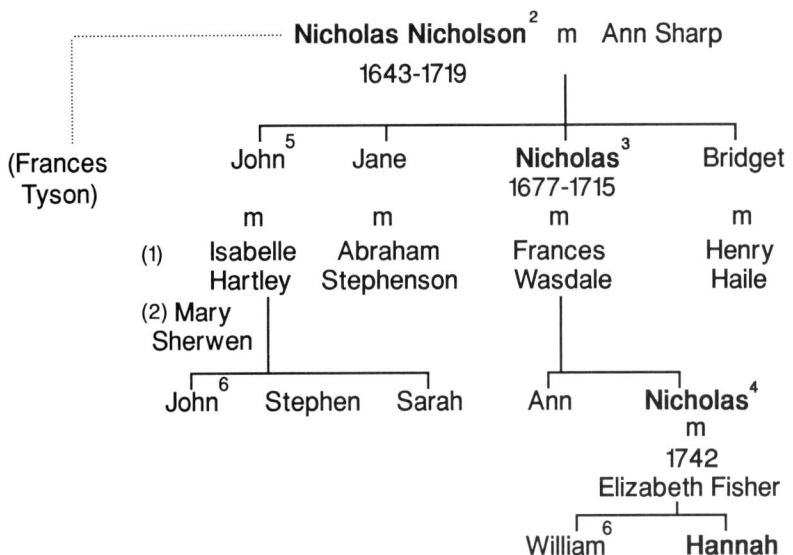

From the tree on the previous page, John[5] and Isabell were at Randlehow where they produced two sons and a daughter, John[6] (b. 1710), Stephen (1711) and Sarah (b.1717). There are many descendants of these three children today, from Illinois to Carlisle, looking for their roots, who, like all family historians, come up against a blank wall now and again.

Bridget and Henry Haile produced four children.

Jane and Abraham Stephenson, one.

Nicholas[3], my ancestor, had two children, Ann and Nicholas[4]. Of Ann I know nothing, but Nicholas[4] married c1742, Elizabeth Fisher at Eskdale. Another ancestor of whom I know little.

In 1759, Nicholas[4] left Yeathouse and a Henry and William Tyson took it over. The next information I have is that Nicholas[4], now of Lowplace, buying Penny Hill and Pyats Nest from John and Dinah Addison of Beckstones (Kirkby Ireleth), Dinah having inherited from her father in 1755. Her mother was formerly Jane Stephenson from Crosbythwaite. In 1763, William[6], son of Nicholas[4], bought Spothow .

On the 27[th.] of April 1768, Nicholas[4] was buried at Eskdale followed by his son William[6] on May 4[th.] of the same year. Elizabeth, Nicholas's widow, was admitted to Penny Hill and William's sister Hannah as his 'sister and heir-at-law', was admitted to Spothow. You will have read about this enfranchising in the Hird chapter. But I came across a little bit more of their history in the 'Transactions of the C & W' in an article by Mary Fair, concerning the discovery, of an Ivory Diptych, during the demolition of Spothow in 1870. Spothow was, by then, in the possession of Hannah's grandchild. There is also a diptych which was in the possession of a person in Ulpha sixty years ago, this I was privileged to see when young and I can vouch for the beautiful craftsmanship of these ivory carvings depicting scenes from the life of Christ.

Describing the location of Spothow, Mary Fair refers to a Bridge 'built by Men Of Grasmere' below Muncaster Castle, but does not give the source of her information nor where she learned that one of the families that lived there I quote 'One Bateman was a Pack-horse driver'. Was it 'my' Henry?

I will give the tree of the last Nicholson of Yeathouse which will
also show yet another Hartley connection. It is true to say they are
intertwined with all the Nicholson families.

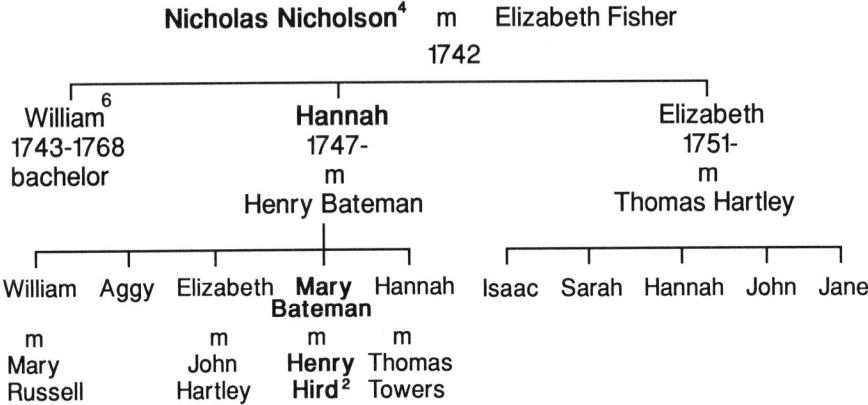

Another Nicholson line leading to the Hirds.

I said Yeathouse was taken over by the Tysons; by 1815 it is refered
to in the registers as Yatthouse, and in 1819 it was called Gatehouse,
still occupied by a blacksmith.

On November 21st. 1846, Henry Hird[5], blacksmith, great-grandson
of Nicholas Nicholson[4] and Elizabeth Fisher, was married at Eskdale
Church, to Elizabeth Rodgers of Hollinghow, and took up residence
at Gatehouse. So once again, Nicholson descendents were back there.
Later, when the Porters took up residence, they gave it back its ancient spelling.

We say 'It's a small world' and we are inclined not to realise that
people in previous generations travelled a lot. In the 1851 census for
Eskdale, who should be visiting Henry[5] but his cousins, *'Henry Hird
U.M. aged 49, shoemaker, Robert Benson U.M. 54 blacksmith, both
born Ambleside'*, this is Henry Hird[4] and his cousin, the two black
sheep of the Hird family!

Nicholsons of Bridge End, Bought (Boot)

I have already remarked about the Hartleys being intertwined with the Nicholsons. Here I have them joined again. From records, I am able to trace the history of Bridge End, in Boot. In recent years, this house was occupied by Arthur Irvine who made shepherds' crooks. After his death, a few years ago, it was sold and turned into a holiday complex.

The earliest date I have found is 1578, when Gilbert Hartley was tenant.

In 1587 in the Heaf & Cow Drifts Gilbert Hartley & John Nicholson.

1627, William Nicholson admitted tenant after the death of his father, Henry.

1633/4 at the General Fine, William Nicholson was admitted by Elizabeth his mother and guardian, late Gilbert Hartley.

1648-69 Fine Book, Henry Nicholson, infant, admitted in 1669, by his guardian, William Jackson.

There is a rental for Henry Nicholson in 1674 and he was there at the General Fine of 1688.

In 1696, William Nicholson was fined and admitted upon the death of his late father; as he had no male heir, he in turn surrendered it to his grandson John Hartley who enfranchised it in 1759.

What do we know of these people? Three Henry Nicholsons died in 1627, two at Bought and one at Hollinghow.

I do not know whose son 'my' Henry[1] was, research might eventually reveal his ancestry, but I do know, from his nuncupative will, that his wife was Elizabeth Viccars, as at the bottom of it is written *'by the oath of William Viccars grandfather to them both'*

Elizabeth remarried in August 1629 and by her second husband, Thomas Nicholson, there were two daughters, Jenet and Isabel. Jenet married Thomas Tyson of Borrowdale Place, bringing yet another Tyson connection into the family.

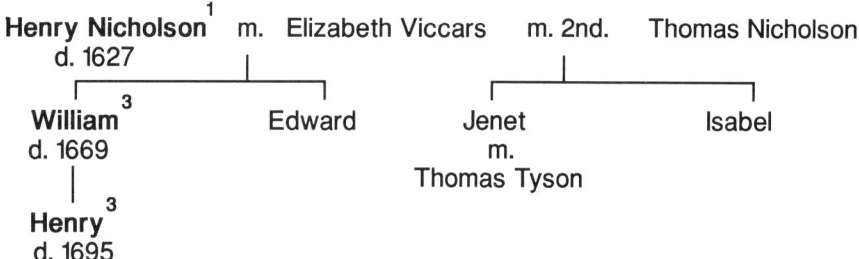

Thomas made his will in 1633. He made his wife Elizabeth and two daughters, Jennett and Elizabeth, Executrixes. (Another example of Isabel and Elizabeth being interchangeable.) What a job they must have had sorting out his affairs, as the will consists of who he owes money to and who owes it to him. It is a wonderful will for names, but a nightmare sorting out relationships. He speaks of his brother-in-law John Vicars. He mentions owing his father-in-law for *'food & Bigg Seven shillings'* and bequeathed six pence to George Hartley, *'to mind me when I am Dead'.*

The Fine Book of 1648-69 shows that Henry Nicholson[3] was admitted to Bridge End as an infant in 1669 by his guardian William Jackson upon the death of his father, William, but little is known of him until his death in 1695.

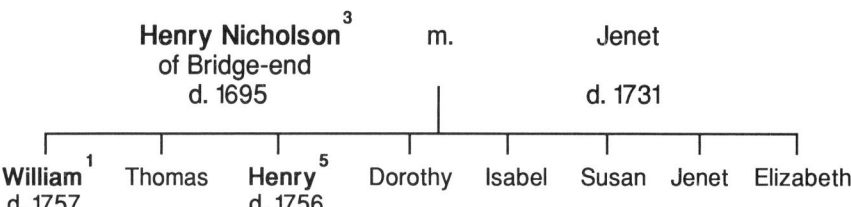

Henry[3] died, leaving estate valued at £91. The valuation was on 12th April 1695, made by John Nicholson, Robert Stephenson, Edward Tyson and Nicholas Hartley. His cattell (sic) were worth £17, his sheep £28, Horses £7 and the Heriot Cow £3.

Let me explain, to those of my readers who are not familiar with the meaning of Heriots. I think John Richardson in his Local Historian's Encyclopedia gives the clearest definition:

'Heriot
An obligation, derived from Saxon times, on an Heir to return to the lord the war apparel of the deceased tenant which had been originally supplied by the lord. The military gear, depending on the

status of the tenant included a horse, harness and weapons. This obligation applied to both freeman and villien. About the time of the Conquest this custom was being superseded by the tenant's heir giving the lord the best beast, and later this simply became a money payment.'

The bond for Henry[2]'s will has also survived and was signed by Jannett Nicholson Widdow (sic), her mark, William Nicholson, both of Ashdale and Thomas Tyson of Wasdale. Was this Thomas her brother or her father? Jenet died in 1731 and left a will. From these two wills, together with the parish registers, I have been able to clarify relationships.

To William[3] she left the proverbial shilling, after all he had, by customary right, got the farm; the same to Thomas, *'if he be living'*, a clause found in many wills of that period making one wonder were these absent people away fighting or were they some of the earliest emigrants. Twenty shillings to Jenet Nicholson and her husband, (Jenet had obviously married a man of the same name.) Twenty shillings to four Tyson grandchildren. (The registers record the burial of Dorothy wife of Thomas Tyson of Cockley Beck on January 23rd 1725). Forty shillings to her daughter, Elizabeth Dickinson (23rd July 1717, William Dickinson married Elizabeth Nicholson at Eskdale). The rest to son Henry and three daughters, Susan Jackson, Elizabeth Dickinson and Isabel Viccars. A very useful will.

Eskdale Mill, (Bridge End in background at the left)
From '*The Northern Tourist*' 1835

Eskdale Mill

William[1] was admitted tenant to Bridge-end at the Manor Court in 1696, the year after the death of his father, Henry[3]. H was the eldest of the eight children, but little is known of his adult life until his two daughters were baptised in Eskdale. There are two marriages in the Eskdale registers of William Nicholsons, either of them, both of them, or neither of them could be his. An Tyson married William Nicholson on November 27th. 1701 and the other one, Ann Wilson on July 27th. 1703. (or he even might have had a clandestine marriage, like his brother Henry). An, Ann and Annas are interchangable with Agnes, the name under which William's wife was buried.

Jane, his elder daughter, who was baptised on July 20th 1703, married Thomas Hartley of Church House. Was it to celebrate this event that William erected the lovely oak screen, still in Bridge End?

William's younger daughter, Dorothy, was baptised on March 17th. 1705. The registers show that she married an Edward Tyson of Bridge-end. I say 'an' because at this time there were six Edward Tysons having children baptised in the valley; fortunately, the parson inserted the addresses.

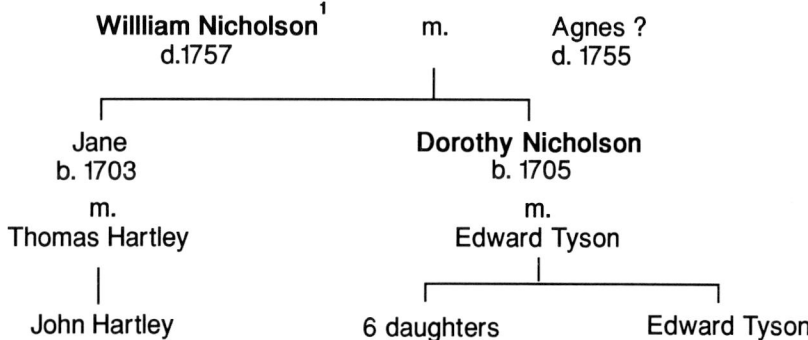

I spent many hours looking for the burials of William and Agnes and once again, got the first clue from Letters of Attorney. On June 4th. 1750, William, now of Hallgarth, constituted Stephen Nicholson of Randlehow, blacksmith, to act as his attorney when he turned Bridge-end over to his grandson John Hartley. William and Agnes were now living with their other daughter and son-in-law Dorothy and Edward Tyson who, for some unknown reason, after having had six daughters baptised at Eskdale, had gone over the tops to Hallgarth in Tilberth-waite where their only son was born. Why had they moved? There had been Tysons living at Hallgarth for many years but I have not found a relationship for Edward with them. Wills are scarce. Agnes Nicholson was buried at Coniston on May 1st. 1755 and William on March 23rd. 1757. Neither left a will.

We now have the following tree showing yet another link with the Hirds.

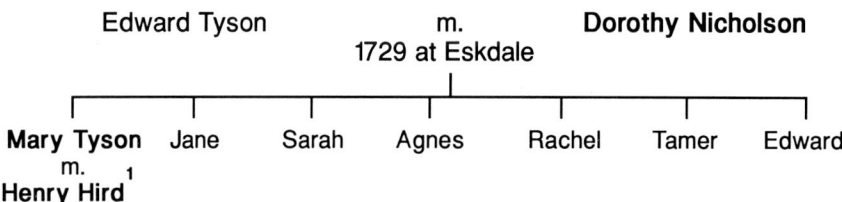

Research shows that William Nicholson's brother, Henry[5], is also one of my ancestors; he died at Sella in Dunnerdale in 1756. At that time there were three dwellings at Sella I have been unable to identify which one Henry occupied, but at a guess think it was possibly the one by the road-side, long a ruin. How Henry Nicholson came to be living there is another mystery as he owned the Crook, Ulpha which in his will he left to his grandson, Henry Tyson, son of his only child Sarah Nicholson by her husband Isaac Tyson.

This Henry Tyson died in 1773 leaving *'my messuage, called Crook, with whole flock of sheep and all the hard goods & furniture that I had bequeath to me by my late Grandfather Henry Nicholson, to my son Henry Tyson'*. It is this Henry Tyson with whom young Henry Hird[2] came to serve his apprenticeship as a blacksmith.

Both Henry Nicholson[5] and Elizabeth his wife are buried at Ulpha, but the only reference to their marriage is the Bishop's Visitation of Eskdale where it is referred to as a *'supposed marriage'* in other words they had been clandestinely married.

Clandestine marriages were common at that period, possibly because the Registration Tax of 1694-99 (see p. 47) when Parliament taxed marriages, births and burials as registered in the parish records, also widowers without children and bachelors. This was a very unpopular tax which led to children not being baptised and marriages being conducted by unscrupulous priests. The Rev. James Stephenson of Seathwaite was notorious for this and was rebuked for disobeying processes from the Court of Richmond. Not all such marriages were solemnised in Churches.

For example, in 1719: *'Septimus Park of Arnaby in Millom married Mary Whinray, they went to a house at Arnaby last Whitsuntide, he hath not shown his Certificate of Marriage nor paid his dues was married (he said) at Kirkby.'* (ARR15/1-39 C.R.O. Preston)

From wills, I have established that Henry Nicholson[5]'s wife Elizabeth, was the daughter of William Dickinson of Harmonthouse, Eskdale, and Alice his wife, who was a daughter of John Viccars of Peel Place. I have yet to research these two families in detail, but from what information I have, a tree can be drawn up, this is shown on the next page.

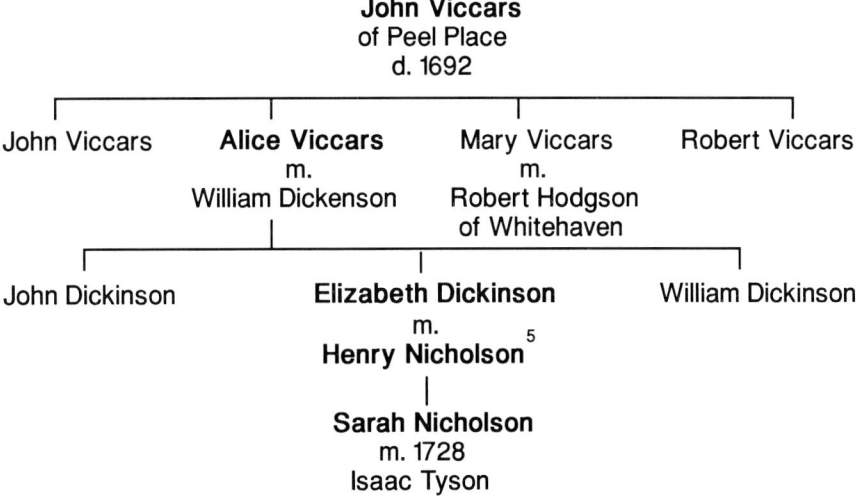

John Viccars
of Peel Place
d. 1692

| John Viccars | **Alice Viccars**
m.
William Dickenson | Mary Viccars
m.
Robert Hodgson
of Whitehaven | Robert Viccars |

| John Dickinson | **Elizabeth Dickinson**
m. [5]
Henry Nicholson | William Dickinson |

Sarah Nicholson
m. 1728
Isaac Tyson

Sarah Nicholson and Isaac Tyson were married at Eskdale on the 10[th.] October 1728 and their daughter Hannah was baptised there on April 17[th.] 1729 when Isaac was *'of Birkerthwaite'*. I have searched for Isaac's baptism to no avail and looked for mention of him in wills and drawn a blank. According to the register, he was of Birkerthwaite the hot bed of the Quakers, so I wonder if he had married out of the Persuasion? He died in 1795 at the Crook, Ulpha, described as *'a weaver aged 90 years'*, and left a very informative will. At the time of his death he was living with his grandson, his son, Henry, having predeceased him.

The tree on the next page has been drawn up from information in Isaac's Will together with the Eskdale registers.

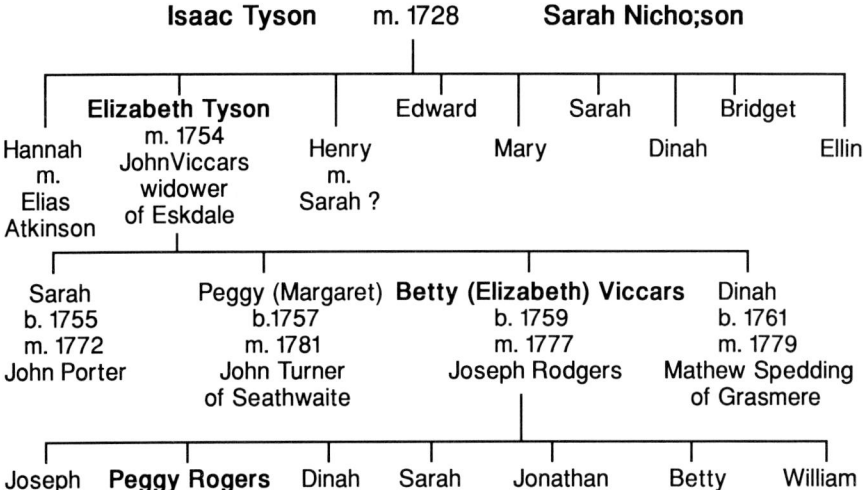

We can now follow this family.

Five of Isaac and Sarah's children died young, Edward, Mary, Sarah, Dinah and Ellin.

Hannah married Elias Atkinson a widower who was described in his father-in-law's will as *'an Apothacary'* and had three daughters.

Elizabeth Tyson, the second daughter, went over the moors to wed John Viccars, also a widower *'of Toes'* (Tawes, Tathes). She is my ancestor and we will concentrate on this family.

Sarah Viccars, Elizabeth's eldest daughter married John Porter, they had thirteen children, including Betty Porter who married the Revd. Edward Tyson of Seathwaite and Margaret, who married the Revd William Powley of Eskdale who also had a large family.

Peggy (or Margaret) Viccars and her husband, John Turner of Hollinhouse in Seathwaite had eleven children including twins.

Dinah Viccars married Matthew Spedding and lived at Blackhall, at the head of the Duddon Valley between 1782 and 1789. They had five children.

My third great-grandparents, Elizabeth Viccars and Joseph Rodgers had seven children. Thus there were at least thirty-six cousins of that generation. (See tree on page 81.)

Joseph and Elizabeth Rodgers were living at Thayes when their first child (Joseph) was born, but were of Brotherilkeld when the rest were baptised. This is the last farm in the Eskdale valley, before the steep climb over Hardknot. Today, like many farms in the area, it is owned by the National Trust; it is farmed by the Harrison family who keep it immaculate. It has a spice cupboard in the kitchen.

It is an impossibility, in a lifetime, to trace everyone in each family, one concentrates on one's own line and notes any interesting information picked up on siblings. Joseph and Elizabeth's eldest daughter Peggy, married Nicholas Stephenson. Their grand-daughter, Margaret Stephenson, married John Hird - these were my grandparents and both were descendants of Henry Nicholson[3] who died in 1695.

Brotherilkeld Farm

Nicholsons in Eskdale in General

That all the Nicholsons in the district were related I am sure, but as yet the available records have not revealed a common ancestor - I live in hope! Neither do we know when the family first went to Yatthouse and Hollinhow.
There are admittances of Henry Nicholson to both places upon the death of his father, William, in The Fine Books 1627 (D/Lec/314/43).

According to wills, a William Nicholson died in 1612, giving *'all the whole title & tenments which I have at Hollinghow & Yeathouse and all the forge gear that my father gave me after my father's decease'* thus bequeathing his expectations, Grandfather Henry died in 1627 mentions his grandson Henry to whom he also leaves *'my Hackney Sadle and my Sword.'* Is this the sword that John Nicholson of Randlehow left in his will in 1717?

Emma Nicholson, who I believe to be Henry's second wife, died the following year, also leaving an interesting will. In it she mentions her brother, Nicholas Jenkinson, the wife of John Casson and a John Dawson, leading me to think that she was from the Duddon Valley.

Obviously this family were blacksmiths as well as farmers. The inventory of goods for William Nicholson (1612), shows items for both occupations but it is of particular interest as it mentions a number of people who owed him money, several of whom lived in Ulpha. Locations are also given. *'Thomas Tyson of Woodend, John Carter of Baskell, John Besbrowne of Bigartmyre, William Atkinson of Low.'* Some was owed by a Nicholas Nicholson of Broadyeat (which is in Thwaites), also by a John Nicholson of Low Place and Nicholas Nicholson of Bought. This last named was one of the appraisers of the inventory.

From these wills I have compiled the tree on the next page.

The most frustrating thing about the wills of Henry (1627) and Emma (1628) is that they refer to William's grand children as the two children of Henry Nicholson and I have not been able to find Henry's will. In my own mind I feel sure that one was Nicholas Nicholson of Randlehow who in 1636 married Bridget Robinson and the other, John of Slapestones, but I cannot prove it.

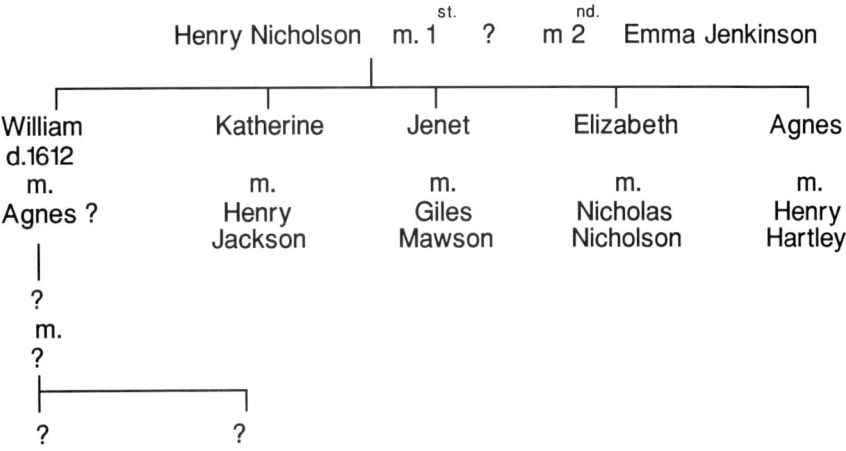

The earliest will I have is dated 1608 and is that of John Nicholson, a yongman (sic) *'sick in my bodie by the visitation of allmightie God'*. He mentions a brother, Henry, a glover, Thomas Hartley son of Gilbert and his master Mathew Kitchen. *'Seven score sheep some part at Cockleybeck'* (Seathwaite) *'some part at Gridall in Wasdall and some part at Paddockwray'* These are valued at £23 - not bad for a youngman! But the most interesting item *'I give to a woman pregnant by me* (will torn) .... *And is with child by me and if it live and she comes to that time according to the .... Nature then I will my father and mother take it and bring it up'*. Snippets of family history, how one would love to know the full story, but is good to know the poor woman was not cast aside. Later on, in Nicholson wills, a Dorothy Nicholson, no relationship ever given, was the legatee of a shilling or two. Was this the child?

From Church records I discovered that the inhabitants borrowed money from both the 'Poor Stock' and the 'Church Stock'. For example, from 5[th.] April 1700 to April 1701, over £29 was loaned out in sums varying from fifteen shillings to seven pounds. A lot of money in so short a time. The conditions of these loans to be repaid on demand with 'Consideration', which later is recorded as 'Lawful Interest'. Those who applied usually had different addresses,

e.g. *'Wee John Wilson of Whoses and Richard Tyson of Hollings both in Eskdale, yeomen, have borrowed of the Chapple Wardens of the Chappellary of Eskdale the summ of twenty shillings of the Chapple Stock'*

Both made their marks and it was witnessed by John Jackson and John Nicholson on 26th October 1699. Most persons were yeomen, exceptions being Nicholas Nicholson, blacksmith and his son, Nicholas Nicholson, who, in the same year, borrowed two pounds of the 'Poor Stock'. Mr. Joseph Porter of Lowholme in Mitredale, Gent and in 1711 Edward Holm and John Tyson, both of Birker, Taylors, borrowed Forty Shillings.

St. Catherine's Church, Eskdale

Social History

That people moved around is a certainty, even if only to neighbouring villages. The debts owing to William Nicholson show that farmers on the tops at Ulpha must have found it more convenient to bring their horses to Eskdale Green for shoeing, rather than go down into their own valley. They would hardly make a detour when taking their wool to Kendal as the main road went via Penny Hill to join the main route over Hardknot and Wrynose.

In wills, legacies are often left to persons *'if they come to claim it'*. Where were these missing persons? We know that a number of people went to London, others went away to Universities graduating as Doctors of Divinity and being given livings in many Southern places. Many young men from both Cumberland and Westmorland went to Queens' College Oxford, founded in 1340 by Robert Eaglesfield of Eaglesfield in Cumberland.

'Robert Eaglesfield, Rector of Brough, Confessor to Queen Philippa and founder of Queen's College, Oxford, was born at Allonby. In 1340, he bequeathed all his lands to the college which was founded for one Provost and twelve Fellows, to be chosen from Cumberland and Westmorland.' (Mannix & Whellan 1847)

There are records from the late c16 showing graduates from both the Nicholson and Porter families of Cumberland. e.g. *'Thomas Nicholson M.A. Adm. Sizar at Queens', June 22, 1594. Of Cumberland. Matric. 1593: B.A. from St.Catherine's 1597-8.'*

Younger sons were often sent away to serve an apprenticeship to every known trade to various parts of the country many to London. In 1710 a stamp duty was imposed on apprenticeship indentures, the records of this tax are in the P.R.O. and cover the period of the tax up to 1811. Indexes of London Apprentices to various trades have been printed and from the Drapers there is in 1641 *'Jas. Ric. Braithwaite of Kendal.'* There are earlier records of Westmorland boys being apprenticed in Bristol, on Feb 5[th.] 1626/7 *'Arthur, son of Solomon Benson, Gent. of Langdale to Barnard Benson, pewterer'.* (I presume a relative.) (Ref. C.R. Hudleston).

From the tax records in 1714, *'John Hicks s. of John of Carlisle, Gent to Thomas Lutwidge, Whitehaven, Merchant.'*

That the yeomen were called up to quell the Scots is seen by the Muster Rolls. The earliest reference I have, is that of 1580/81 with lists of names of the villages and those called up for North Cumberland and North Westmorland. These can be seen in the Calender of Border Papers. Unfortunately, I have not found those for the south of the counties. However, I came across a document giving the names and equipment of some men called up for *'Lord Lonsdale Regiment of Trainbands for Cumberland & Westmorland'* during the 1745 rebellion.

Humphrey Senhouse, Capt.

Francis Irwin		*Wm. Smith*	
Wm. Woodburn	*Sergts.*	*Thomas Tyson*	*all three*
Robert Barret *drummer*		*William Johnson*	*Corpalls*

Weapons

Ulpha	*Thomas Jackson*	*a bad Pike, a bad Sword*
	Thomas Tyson	*a bad pike, an old Sword*
	John Whinfield	*a bad Musket, an old Sword*
Eskdale	*Wm. Dickinson*	*a bad Musket, a bad Sword*
Wasdale	*John Fletcher*	*a bad musket, a bad Sword*
Netherwasdale	*Henry Tyson*	*a good Musket, a good Sword*
Irton & Santon	*John Nicholson*	*a bad Musket, an old Sword*
	John Dixon	*a good Musket, an old Sword*

All these men had belts, mostly bad ones.   (PR/Eskdale)
Not very well equipped!

I have just given some reasons for people leaving their homes and where they might go. Doubtless many also went to sea.

Whitehaven had become a substantial port by 1685, when a survey of the numbers of *'Families & Inhabitants'* was taken; the result was 268 families and 1089 Inhabitants. A few years later another church was built to accommodate all these people. It was not completed until 1715, but I have documents dated 29[th.] May 1708 and 31[st.] May 1708 referring to the *'Building of the New Church at Whitehaven'* and the sale of the pews. This apparently provided a means of making money at an almost unbelievable rate, as on the 29[th.] Andrew Pellin bought seat number 85 for £6.10s. and two days later sold it to James Milham for Ten Pounds!

Disputes arose between tenants, and between Lords of the Manors which often led to law suits. To save the journeys to wherever these suits were being held, witnesses made depositions, giving their names, ages and addresses, how long they had lived there and a lot more valuable historical information.   There was a suit between the Sharpes and the Tysons of Eskdale in the late 1700s and another between the Lord of Millom and the Lord of Birker and Austhwaite about the same time.

Wood was of great value, as so much was needed to build ships, especially warships and surveys of the trees were carried out at regular intervals. In 1627, the five tenements in Myterdale had between them 4,101 trees, which included 1,181 on Nicholas Stephenson's land.

Doctor Bridge, Eskdale

CASSON ANCESTORS (SELLA)

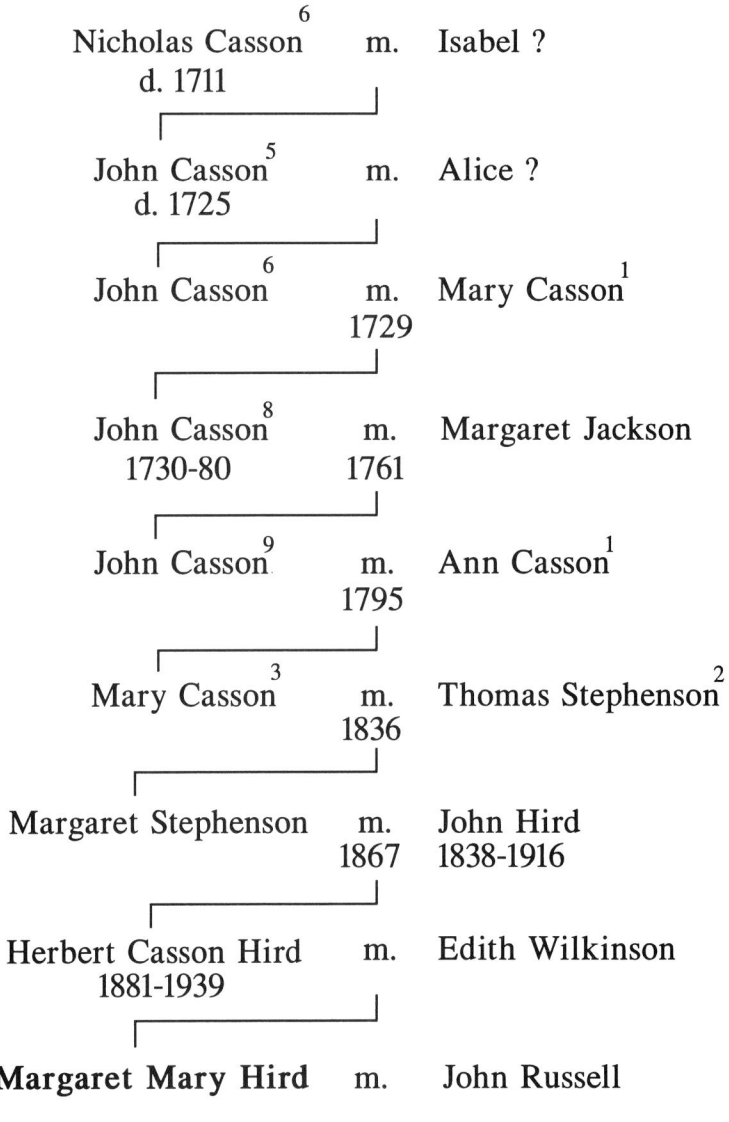

Nicholas Casson[6]   m.   Isabel ?
d. 1711

John Casson[5]   m.   Alice ?
d. 1725

John Casson[6]   m.   Mary Casson[1]
1729

John Casson[8]   m.   Margaret Jackson
1730-80   1761

John Casson[9]   m.   Ann Casson[1]
1795

Mary Casson[3]   m.   Thomas Stephenson[2]
1836

Margaret Stephenson   m.   John Hird
1867   1838-1916

Herbert Casson Hird   m.   Edith Wilkinson
1881-1939

Margaret Mary Hird   m.   John Russell

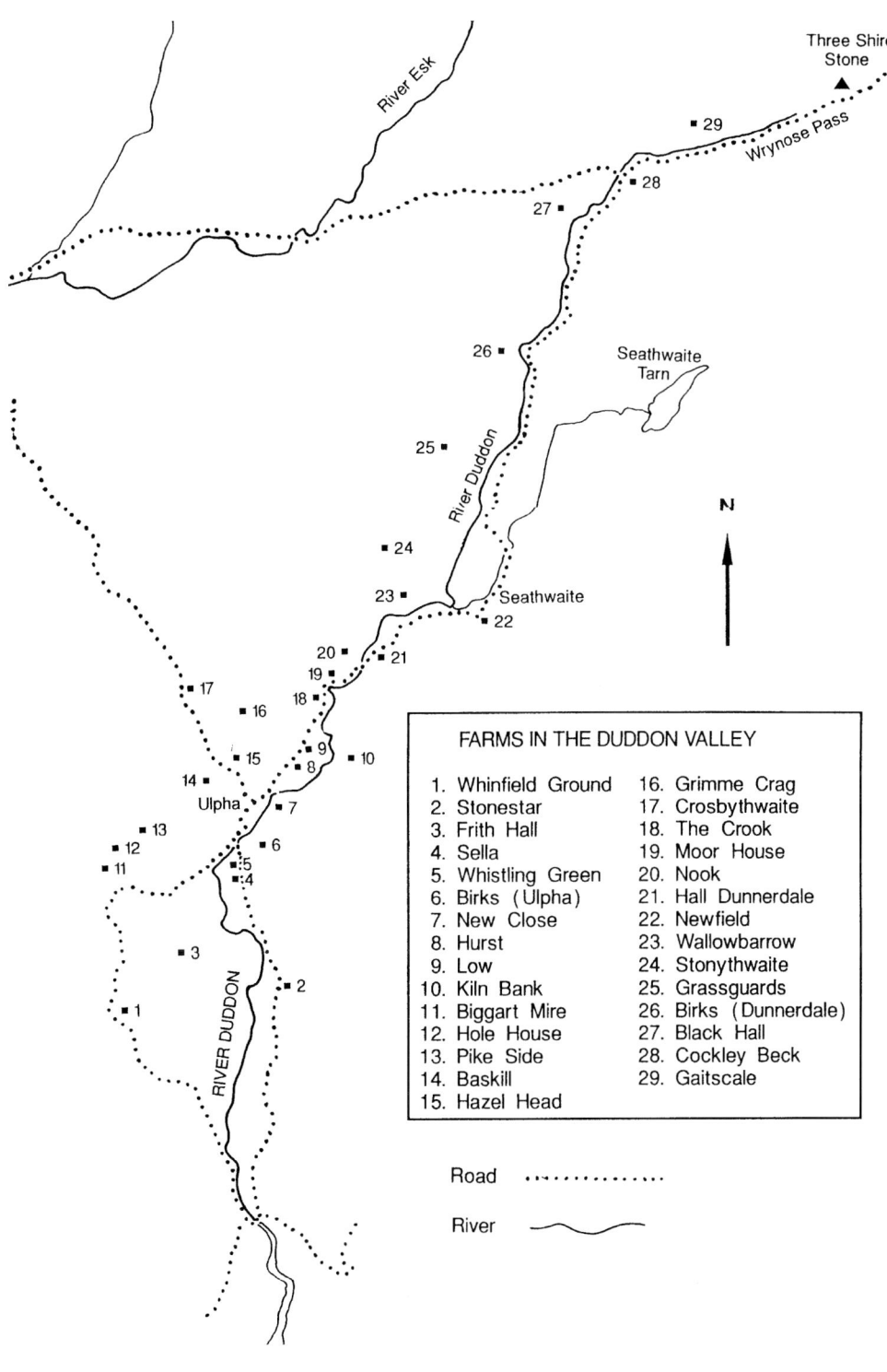

FARMS IN THE DUDDON VALLEY

1. Whinfield Ground
2. Stonestar
3. Frith Hall
4. Sella
5. Whistling Green
6. Birks (Ulpha)
7. New Close
8. Hurst
9. Low
10. Kiln Bank
11. Biggart Mire
12. Hole House
13. Pike Side
14. Baskill
15. Hazel Head
16. Grimme Crag
17. Crosbythwaite
18. The Crook
19. Moor House
20. Nook
21. Hall Dunnerdale
22. Newfield
23. Wallowbarrow
24. Stonythwaite
25. Grassguards
26. Birks (Dunnerdale)
27. Black Hall
28. Cockley Beck
29. Gaitscale

Road   ··············

River   ‿‿‿‿

To the Duddon

Oh, dear old smiling river
I love thy silvery sheen,
I love thy pleasant murmur,
It speaks of what has been.
It speaks of years departed,
Of loved ones passed away,
Of hours of fairy gladness
In childhood's happy play.

I loved to watch in sunshine
The sparkle on thy face,
And in the storm and tempest
Thy wild tumultuous race.
From the old chamber window
I gazed enchanted, awed,
While billows rolled and tumbled
Upon their homeward road.

Of friends who then were near us,
How few, alas, remain
And changes ever meet us,
But thou art still the same.
Still thy pellucid waters
Flow on to meet the sea
And bless the dear old valley
Which gains more charm from thee.

E.P. Eskdale
May 19th. 1905

(Eleanor Porter née Dawson - see p. 73)

PART 4 - THE CASSONS

Casson Ancestry, early years.

My great grandfather, Thomas Stephenson[2], married Mary Casson[3] in 1836; she was a descendant of one of the oldest families in the Duddon valley, as was Thomas's grandmother Margaret Atkinson wife of William Stephenson[2]. Both these families appear in the earliest records of the Seigniory of Millom beginning in the reign of Henry VIII, 1510, and are the earliest which I have been able to find.

These two families of ancestors seem to have been well established in the Duddon Valley at this time, whereas my other forebears came to live there, either by marriage, apprenticeship or change of tenure. In this valley I lived for the first twenty-two years of my life and it will for ever be 'home' to me. My roots are deep, so before I give the family history I will give some for the valley.

On the south side of the Duddon's banks is the village of Seathwaite-with-Dunnerdale, formerly in the County Palatine of Lancaster. On the north side, the village of Ulpha in Cumberland, (pre 1974) while at the top of the valley, the old county of Westmorland meets them at the landmark known as the 'Three Shire Stone' on Wrynose Pass. (See map on page 2.) Here also, meet the old parishes of Millom, Kirkby Ireleth, Ulverston and Grasmere. The main trade road from the coast at Ravenglass was over Wrynose to Ambleside and Kendal.

There were three manors within the valley; a small one, according to County History of Lancashire, of Cockley Beck; a larger one of Seathwaite with Dunnerdale, and finally, Ulpha, which was within the Seigneury of Millom. (The name Seathwaite refers strictly to the valley from the tarn to the Chapel and includes the houses and farms leading to Cockley Beck). Three farms on the Ulpha side at the top of the valley, Gaitskill, Black Hall and Birks, whilst in the Manor of Ulpha, belonged to the Pennington's of Muncaster as referred to on pages 24 and 53. The Manor of Dunnerdale is mentioned circa 1160 (Pipe Roll 311) It was in the hands of the Earl of Derby from circa 1336 but sold in 1610 to the Heskeths. Later it came into the possession of John Penny of Penny Bridge. It was sold to Richard Towers of Duddon Hall (Ulpha) and finally purchased in 1903 by Mr. G.H. Cheetham. Very few documents are available for research.

The only reference I have found to the Manor of Cockley Beck, is in the C&W Trans. NS viii concerning sheepgates made in 1681.

The Manor of Ulpha was held by the Hudlestons of Millom, then eventually belonged to Sir James Lowther Bart. The records are extensive, and from these I have drawn much local, social and family history. We family historians are greatly indebted to the Lonsdale and Leaconfield estates for making their wonderful collections available.

There was a Church at Seathwaite from very early times, reputedly built by an Earl of Derby, to ease the long journey of taking corpses to Kirkby, though probably only a Chapel of Ease within the Parish of Kirkby Ireleth and tied up with the parish of Broughton with whom the Seathwaite parishioners were always falling out.

The parish of Kirkby Ireleth belonged to the Dean and Chapter of York, and was known as a 'Peculiar', so Wills of this parish had to be proved there and applications for marriage licences the same. The records of both are in The Borthwick Institute, York. It is interesting to read the report of the 1649 Church Survey, enacted, that on and after the 29th. March of that year the *'Name, title, dignity, function and office of Dean, Sub-dean, Dean and Chapter and or Collegiate Church'* in England and Wales, should be abolished; and that all lands or other possessions which then or within ten years before the beginning of the then Parliament, of right belonging to any such church dignitary, should be vested in certain trustees, who were to sell the same, after having first had a survey. The following was for the parish of Kirkby Ireleth:

'And ye said Jurors further say upon their Oaths, That ye Parish Church of Kirkby Ireleth (ye longitude of ye said Parish being Ten Miles and latitude Two miles, and Ye Church seated within a mile and a half of ye East end of ye said parish) is a Viccarage' (sic) *'presentative by ye Dean and Chapter of York, The Rectory or Tithes of Corne, Wool, lamb and calf being impropriate to ye said Deane and Chapter, and by them farmed to Anthony Laitus, Esq. And That ye same impropriacon is about worth Sixty pounds, out of which is yearly paid to ye poor Thirteen shillings four pence: as also That ye said parish of Kirkby Irleth containeth several Townships hereafter expressed, being distant from their parish Church as followeth; viz, Kirkby Ireleth, being ye place where the Church is seated, Broughton, distance four miles, Seathett eight miles, Dunderdale six miles and Woodland four miles.*

And the Jurors say That there beloneth to ye said Vicarage a Vicarage house and about Two acres of Glebeland, And that there is only a little Tyth hay, hemp, flax, pigg, goose and Bees, which are worth about Twelve pounds p Ann., And whereof ye Vicar takes ye Church-

yard as pt of payment, ye same' (being worth about) *'thirty shillings per ann.*

And the said Jurors say that ye parish of Kirkby Ireleth hath within it severall Chappells (sic) hereafter mentioned, being distant from the parish Church, viz Broughton, which is parochiall, distant as aforesaid four miles, Woodland four miles, Seathett Eight Miles: That there is no Minister or Incumbent at ye parish Church, but ye place void by death of Mr. Askew, late Vicar. And the said Jurors further say, That ye several Chapples situated within ye said parish of Kirkby Ireleth are provided of Maintainance and Ministers as hereafter followeth: viz.
   Ye Chapple of Broughton hath Ten pounds p. ann in small Tythes, as also Forty pounds p. ann. Augmentacon by Order from ye Committee of Lancashire for the of ye Rents of ye Earl of Derby in Furness: The Minister Mr. Thomas Rigby, Master of Arts, Officiating there for the time being, The Chappel of Woodland hath no Maintainance, but only what ye people there inhabiting please to contribute to a Reader. And ye Chappel of Seathet hath ye like. The parishioners humbly pray That a competent Maintainance may be allowed and Godly Masters for yr said Church and Chappels'

No wonder there was disagreement between Seathwaite and Broughton.

Likewise a Church at Ulpha and from the manorial records it is possible to find names for some of the early priests. This church was attached to that of Millom.

At the *'Court Bierlage holden in the name and to the use of John Hudleston on 26th. April, Third year of the Reign of King Henry VIII* (1511) *Before George Midleton Steward of the court'* there came fifty-eight tenants to pay their tax. Many of the names long gone from the area such as Cockenscail, sometimes written as Cockenstall, or Twisaday, in this list is given John Fell, Chaplain.

At the Manorial Court of the same year, a John Crudson was presented for breaking the peace upon Robert Cook, Chaplain at the Chapel of St. John Baptist. Were there two Chaplains or did John Fell just own the tenement or pay to pasture sheep? In this document is the first mention of the name Casson, when Richard Casson was presented for breaking into the house of John Logan and also for drawing blood on the said John. Not a good start to your ancestors! The Atkinsons were better behaved! It was a time when there appeared to be much thieving and fighting but also a time when customs were being enforced and boundaries defined. More of that later.

As Cassons married Cassons, it is difficult to know where to begin. They were all connected, that is those from Sella, Birks, New Close, Kilnbank, Hall Dunnerdale, Grimme Cragg, Frith Hall and New Field, of that I am sure, and there would also be connections with those in Broughton.

The first list of manorial tenants I have is dated 1577, when the manor was still in the possession of the Earls of Derby. It names Roger Casson and Thomas Casson as two of the tenants.

There is a mention of Nicholas Casson of 'Sellow' in the inventory of J....... Cooper, yeoman, of Thwaites in 1598, whoe owed money to Nicholas. Is this the Nicholas Casson whose will was proved in 1624?

'Nicholas Casson of Sellah

He desired to be buried at Broughton in Furness his temporall goods to be disposed of as followth:
first I give unto Nicholas my son one chest:
Itm I give unto the three daughters of my brother Thomas Casson two lambs:
I give unto the said Thomas .... Doublet:
I give unto my brother John one peare (sic) *of blue britches and unto his son one lambe'*
There are one or two small legacies to people and he contiues: *'Ex-ecutrix of this my last Will and testament I ordain and make Ellen my Wife, she paying my debts and Funeral Expences according to the law'* ....Will torn *'and I make George Carter my cousen* (sic) *and Thomas Casson my brother supervisors.'* Witnesses were Thomas Casson, Nicolas Dicconsone and George Carter. Probate was granted to Ellena Casson de Sellow, Thomas Casson[1] of New Close and George Carter de Ulpha.
Was this Thomas Casson the one who went to Grimme Cragg? (page 62)

Nicholas Casson[1]'s goods were appraised by James Dawson, Thomas Wilkinson, John Casson and Rowlande Casson, (another name I am unable to fit into the family), and were valued at *'XXXiijs Ivd'* (33s/4d) they included a clock, brass and pewter. His total estate was valued at the sum of *'XXXj Is Xjs'*, (£31.11s.) but even more interesting is a list of sixty people who owed him money. Included among the debtors was the curate, the Reverend Peter Chamberlaine whose debt was fifteen shillings. What was Nicholas Casson's occupation to have so much money out in debts. Did he act as a banker, money lender or was he perhaps a tradesman? So many unanswered questions arise when recording family history.

From this will can be drawn up the first of the many Casson trees

Casson - Tree 1.

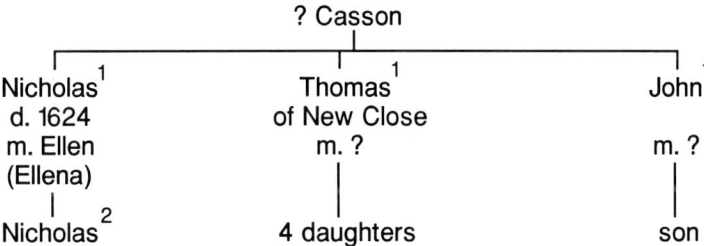

? Casson

Nicholas[1]	Thomas[1]	John[1]
d. 1624	of New Close	
m. Ellen	m. ?	m. ?
(Ellena)		
Nicholas[2]	4 daughters	son

In his will of 1667, Roger Casson of Hall Dunnerdale desires to be buried at Broughton. He leaves all the loose wood and boards belonging to the house to his son Thomas[2]. To son John[3] *'ten of my best sheep' at Sella in my brother John* [(2)]*'s keeping'*, to his daughters Elizabeth and Ellen *'my sheep in Edward Jackson's possession'* and also £10 to daughter Ellen. As was the custom, a third part of the remainder went to his wife Jennet. He made his daughters executrixes and Joseph Casson of Kilnbank and Thomas Casson[4], younger, of Sella supervisors.

Casson - Tree 2

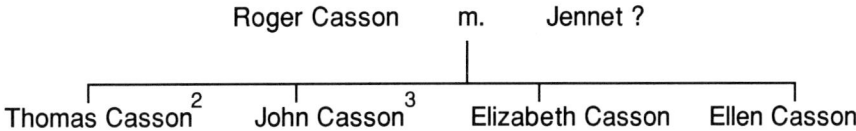

Roger Casson m. Jennet ?

| Thomas Casson[2] | John Casson[3] | Elizabeth Casson | Ellen Casson |

His goods were appraised by John Tyson, Thomas Lordow, Nicholas Walker, and yet another Casson, this time Nicholas. They were worth £64, including the remainder of his sheep with Thomas Fleming, given to his wife Jenet and valued, like those in Edward Jackson's possession, at £1.16.8, while those at Sella were worth £1.13.4. The final reckoning, after debts and legacies had been paid was a surplus of £57.14.8, yet the executrixes had borrowed £1.10s to pay for his funeral. One wonders why. And why were his sheep with other people?

The following year, (1688) Thomas Casson[3] the elder, of Sella, died. His will is worthy of mention.

'*In the name of God Amen: the xij of February Anno Domi 1677 I Thomas Casson the elder of Sella in Dunnerdale,*' followed by the usual preamble...... '*First I give unto my son Nicholas Casson* [4] *all tables, chests, arkes, Chairs, wood and wooden Vessel not hindering his mother of the use of them while she remaineth in the house:*
Itm. I give to my Godson Thomas Jackson two shillings or else one lamb.
Itm. I give to Thomas Besbrown Daughter two shillings or one lamb:
Item. I give to Thomas Pret' (Prit) a '*white waistcoat a shirt, a pair of britches and a coat*
Item. I give to my Brother Nicholas Casson [3] *one broadcloth Doublet:*
Item. I give to my five servants either of them one hog.
Item. I give one hog to Anthony Dickson
Itm I give old Fox wife in Broughton sixpence.
Item I give Ellen Innman and Agnes Pennington and widdow (sic) *Woodend each of them vid.*
I give to Elizabeth and Emmet Stephenson either of them vid.
I give to Henry James wife 4d.
Itm I give to Hugh Dickinson one old coat
Itm. I give to my godson Thomas Casson one lamb
I give to Elizabeth Pret one lamb.
Itm. I give to my two grandchildren Thomas Casson [5] *and Elizabeth Casson his his sister A .... will torn....... of Sheep at Birks equally between them.*
Itm I give to my daughter Jane Fleming one Calf
Itm I give to John Pythuwet (?) *tutor two shillings or one lamb.*
Itm. I give to my Brother John Casson [4] *ten shillings and sixpence of the money he is owing me.*
Itm. I give to John Carters wife 4d
And all the rest of my goods unbequeathed I give to my son Nicholas Casson making him and appointing him my whole Executor of this my last Will and Testament he discharging all my just Debts Legacies Funeral Expences according, desiring him to see my Last Will and Testament well and truly performed.

In witness etc. etc. signed and sealed Thomas Casson. Witnesses, (both sign) *Thomas Casson and Thomas Denny.*'
Bonds were signed by Nicholas Casson of Dunnerdale, William Towers of Broughton and Thomas Casson of Dunnerdale.

This is the will of a kind and thoughtful person, it is full of names and relationships, together with interesting descriptions of clothing.

Sella

Before we deal with the inventory we can construct a tree starting with the three known brothers.
Was the Roger who died the previous year another brother?

Casson - Tree 3

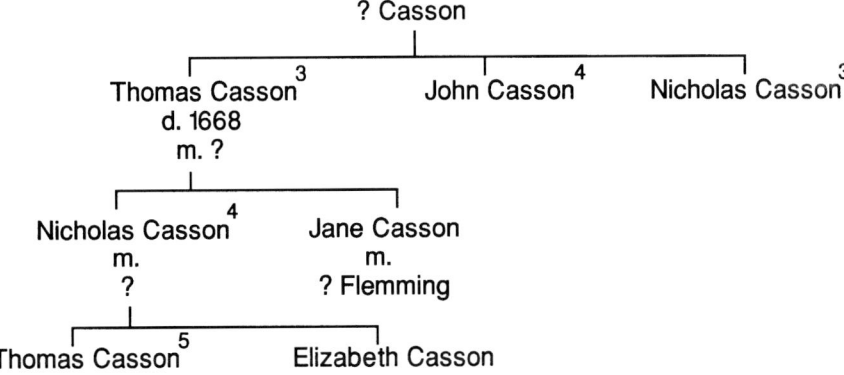

Thomas[3] appears to have been a man of substance, with goods valued at £63 and only £4.16.1d in debts. His goods included garden spades and peat spades. He had beasts worth £21, sheep £10, horses £2 and bees worth £1. As bees were worth no more than two shillings a hive, he must have produced a lot of honey. He also possessed bedding and bedstocks to the value of £4.10, far in excess of the usual goods of the average person of that period.

There were at least three tenements at Sella. One has long been in ruins. Upper Sella, now known as Whistling Green, has been rebuilt and extended, but was previously in a ruinous state and had obviously only been a small place. The third was the 'big' house, where I assume Thomas lived. This house still stands today, Casson descendants still own and occupy it. With its thick walls and a chimney wide enough for smoking hams, it must have been built early 16c if not before. It had a well for its supply of water.

In 1664 a dispute arose between the tenants of Low Sella and Over Sella (was this Upper Sella?), no names are given, but they appeared before the manor court for settlement. The arguments concerned two summer Closes, smitting their sheep and possessing their houses. The findings were as follows:-

'That all the houses, buildings and every part and parcel therof upon Low Sella shall remain with the tenant, his heirs, assigns for ever. The same for Over Sella.'
(Did the tenements have more than one house? If so, it could account for Cassons who I cannot fit into any pedigree through manorial records or wills.)
'The tenant of Low Sella shall smitt their sheep with a cross of Rode and Over Sella with a cross of Waddie both upon the shoulder, failing to do so a fine of 3s 4d for each default.
The said tenants shall have either half the Low and High Closes equally between them: from the 15[th.] day of April unto the first day of November yearly in Summer and from the first day of November unto the 15th of April their goods shall go in both Closes horn for horn without any differences. Again failing to do 2s for every default. That the tenant of Low Sella shall not let his goods belonging to Birks to feed willingly on the Common Pasture belonging to Over Sella, for every default 3s.4d.'

Both tenants were bound in £100, which was a considerable sum at that time.

I am unable to construct any trees for the following years until early the following century, when Thomas Casson[6] of Upper Sella died in 1706, and Nicholas Casson[6] of Sella in 1711/12.

From Thomas's will I can compile a tree:

Casson - Tree 4

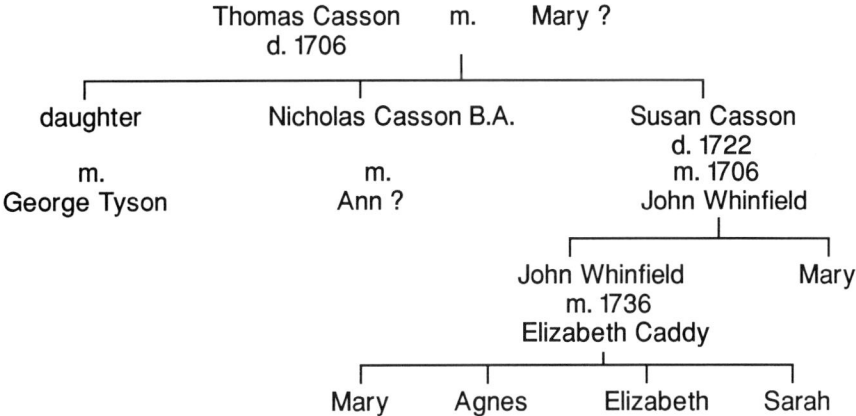

Thomas left a simple will which was proved by his son Nicholas[5] and Christopher Wallas of Kirkby Kendal (whom we shall meet again in the next will), but a very interesting inventory. Amongst the goods, which included husbandry gear, was a whip saw and other instruments belonging to a carpenter. Total £30. 09.11 He was owed money by several people. The list of debtors is interesting as it indicates where a number of people lived.

Debts owing to deceased without Speciality

John Jackson of Wallowbarrow	*£1.0.0*
Thomas Jackson of Crook	*£1.0.0*
Elizabeth Gibson of Grime Cragg	*10s.*
Wm. Myers of Hillend	*£1.15s.*
John Casson of Kilnbank	*12s.*

Thomas Casson[6]'s debts amounted to £5.10s which included £2.1.3d to Nicholas Casson for a cow, and 5s.2d to the minister. His total clear assets were £64.17.7d, so he was another quite wealthy person.

Of his children, the daughter who married George Tyson had four daughters, Mary, Agnes, Elizabeth and Sarah. I have done no research on these, but I have no doubt they would belong to the top end of the valley.

His daughter Susan, married John Whinfield and died in 1722, leaving a son John and a daughter Mary. John, (1707-82) was married in 1736 to Elizabeth Caddy; research is being done by their descendants. Quite recently I came across a Jackson will which indicated that Susan (née Casson) and John Whinfield are my seventh great-grandparents as will be shown later when following another Casson branch. I have not researched Susan's daughter, Mary.

At the time of his father's death, Nicholas[5] was studying in Dublin. From   the 'IAlumni Dublinensis' I discovered, *'Siz. (Mr. W. Lancaster) August 26th. 1703, son of Thomas, Carpentarius, b. Co Lancaster, B.A. Vern 1708'* He became a clergyman.

[A Sizar was a student at Cambridge or Dublin receiving a college allowance towards his expenses. Was Mr. Lancaster his tutor? Did 'B.A.Vern' indicate that he studied in English rather than Latin?]

No mean achievement for the son of a carpenter. I wonder who was his teacher before he went to University? His studies would be done by rush candles, made from mutton fat.

From some old deeds: *'11th. June 1733, Deed Poll from Nicholas Casson of South Clifton, Nottinghamshire, Clergyman, to John Casson of High Sella, Blacksmith,'* being a conveyance of a tenement of High Sella of the yearly rent of 5s.4d. 8th. August 1734 John Casson admitted tenant. What was the relationship between the two?

11th. July 1734, Indenture between the last named John Casson[7] of the one part and Mary Casson[1] his niece, of Low Herst in Ulpha in the County of Cumberland, on the other part, being conveyance of the said Tenement at High Sella.

9th. October 1734, Mary Casson admitted. Mary was the daughter of Robert Casson of Hall Dunnerdale, so John must have been his brother, unless Robert had married a Casson as frequently happened.

The next will, that of Nicholas Casson[6] of Sella, was made in 1700 but proved in 1711/12 by John Casson[5] of Ulpha, yeoman, William Dixon of the same and Thomas Casson of Dunnerdale. Nicholas was not as wealthy as some of his kinsfolk. From it I am able to draft the tree shown on the next page.

Çasson - Tree 5

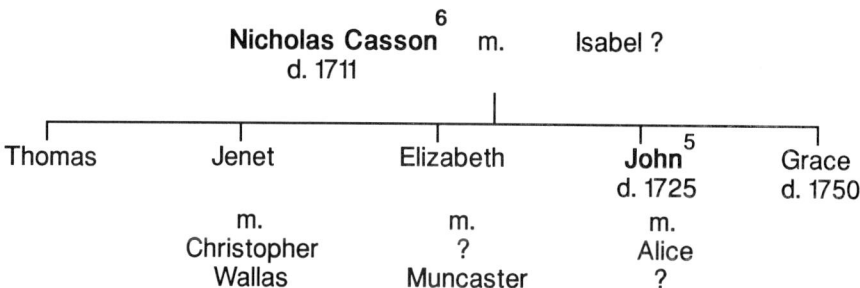

Nicholas[6], though giving his residence as Sella, left to his eldest son and heir Thomas, his *'Estate of land at Birks'* there is no mention of a tenement at Sella. To his younger son, John[5], my ancestor, he left the remainder of his goods to be shared with his sister Grace, whom John was charged to educate and bring up.

John[5] had bought Low Herst, Ulpha a few years earlier. This was not the house that stands today, but was one on the right side of the road going up the valley, it fell into ruins early last century (20th.). This was where my grandmother was born. Later, the house was completely destroyed for widening the road. John[5] was the second Casson that I know of who crossed the Duddon to live in Ulpha, the other being Thomas who bought Grimme Cragg. By this time there were a number of families of Cassons in the valley. The Protestation Returns of 1641/2 name two Johns, two Thomases, two Isabells and one widow. One of the Johns was from Panel Holme and there was a Thomas at Grimme Cragg, but by 1700 there were families at Frith Hall, Cat Holes and Panel Holme whom I have been unable to trace back.

John[5] married Alice ?; he died in 1725 leaving her with debts of £5.3.6d. Only his inventory survives. She died ten years later, in 1735 leaving a good and interesting will. She had obviously cleared the debts as she left money to her daughters and to her son John[6]:

'I give and bequeath unto my son John Casson all the Loose Wood lying in the barn and one Ark one Cupboard and a Table and also the Loft over my now Dwelling House together with all the Rafters and likewise Plow and Plow Gear'.

John[6] had married in 1729 so his mother must have moved into a cottage, I think that there were several dwellings at Low Herst. I have drawn up a tree:

Casson - Tree 6

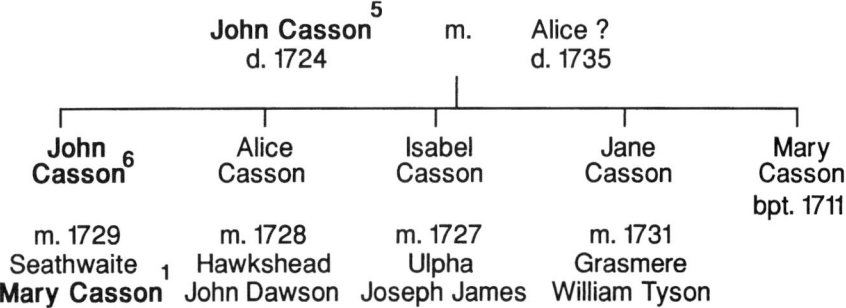

As they married so far away, it is probable that Alice and Jane were in service. Isabel married a local man, Joseph James. The James family had been in Ulpha certainly from 1640 (when one Lawrence James was admitted tenant of Biggardmire) and later, another member of this family married into the Cassons.

Low Hurst

We must now cross the river back to Dunnerdale and Seathwaite, where John[6] married Mary Casson[1] in 1729. I have constructed Mary's tree with the help of the wills of her father and uncles and some research:

Casson - Tree 7

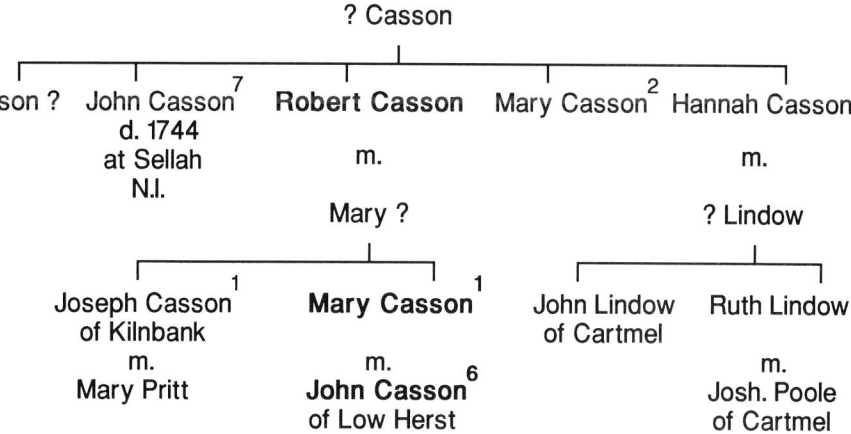

Robert Casson, in his will made in 1744, mentions a granddaughter, Hannah, who must have been Mary's eldest daughter and possibly his first granddaughter, (was that why she was singled out?), son Joseph at Kilnbank, daughter Mary Casson[1] and her other children John, Ferdinando, Mary, Alice, and Dinah.

However, John Casson[7] the blacksmith (1744) left a will worthy of further study.

'John Casson of Sellah in Dunnerdale'
After the preamble he disposes his goods as follows:
'To my Brother Robert Casson I give and bequeath the sum of £10 in money and also one Riding Coat being part of my Apparrel
To my Nephew Joseph Casson [(1)] *son of my said Brother Robert Casson I give and bequeath One Wringer, two pair of Bedsteads and a Table at Kilnbank one Bible and all the loose wood at Kilnbank.*
To my Nephew John Casson I give and bequeath one Plough and the Irons thereto belonging, two pair of double gear and one Iron Harrow and all the loose wood belonging to me at Sellah; One Flesh Cupboard one Riding Coat a Pair of Breeches of Shop-Cloth and one Belt.

To my servant Alice Dawson (see tree No.7) *I give and bequeath the Sum of five pounds in Money and any one cow she thinks proper to Choose out of my Stock.*
To my sister Mary Casson[2] *I give and bequeath one Shilling in Money.* (what had she done to get just the proverbial shilling?)
To my God Son Roger Walker I give and bequeath one Close bodied Coat of Shop Cloth
I also order and appoint and it is my mind and Will that my Executor or Executrix give to every Man or Woman, three pence apiece, who are Invited to my Funeral to be spent at such places as I have directed my servant Alice Dawson
All the residue, and remainder of my goods Chattells, Credits, Money and personal Estate whatsoever, I give and bequeath to my Nephew John Lindow and my Niece Ruth Poole making them Joint Executor and Executrix of this my last will and Testament, they paying all my Funeral Expences' etc. etc.
Witnesses John Casson, Sworn, John Gunson, Robert Walker.
Bond: 24 December 1744 John Lindow Woodmonger, Ruth Poole wife of Joshua Poole, Yeoman both of Moorhow in the Parish of Cartmel and County Palatine of Lancaster and John Casson of Lowhurst in Ulpha in the Parish of Millom County of Cumberland. John Lindow and John Casson both signed and Ruth Poole made her mark. The Estate was valued at £249.18s. So he was a very rich man.

It is noticable that his niece, Mary Casson[1] is not mentioned in the will. Was that because he had already turned his tenement at Sella over to her?

Some of the Cassons seemed to move away from the valley, especially the women. Sella, Kilnbank, Hall Dunnerdale, New Close and Birks seemed to be connected both in ownership and kinship.

Low Hurst Cassons

John[6] and Mary Casson[1] produced a large family. One wonders how they all slept as most of the houses were small.

Casson - Tree 8

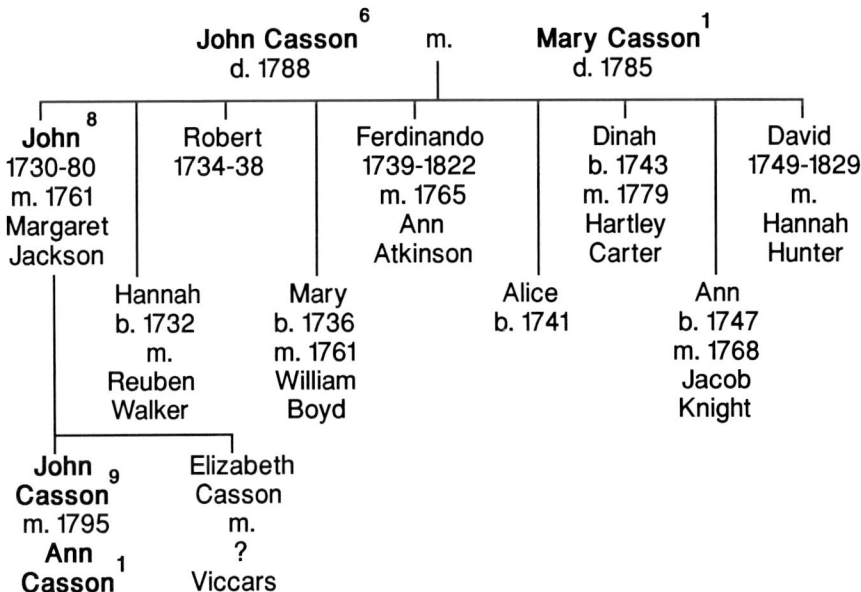

John and Mary prospered; John had business interests as well as farming, he raised a large family and when he died in 1788, he left £139.15s. His inventory is very short:

'Purse & Apparrel £4. Tables etc. £1 Husbandry Utensils 5s. Sheep £30 Owing to deceased upon Security £100 and Rents £4.10s.'

His will does not specify what properties the rents were from except that he left *'all my whole Flock or Stock of Sheep going upon and belonging to my Customary Messuage and tenement at Sellah in Dunnerdale'* to son Ferdinando[1]. This was the tenement given to John's wife Mary by her uncle John[7].

Of this large family, Robert died in infancy and John[8], (my ancestor), Mary and Alice all predeceased their father.

John[8] married Margaret Jackson of Holehouse; they had two children, John[9] and Elizabeth, (Betty), who married a Viccars from Eskdale!

Jacksons

There were several families of Jacksons in the valley from early times; like the Cassons all would be kinsfolk. For years, I had no idea from which family of Jacksons Margaret's father, William, was descended, as there were families living on both sides of the river at Wallowbarrow, Law, and Hazel Head. Those from the Crook were Quakers and the Jacksons from one of the two tenements at New Close, might also have been of that persuasion and have given the small piece of land for their Burial Ground. However, of this I had no proof.

Recently, I found the will of William Jackson of Hazel Head (1823), which is a family historian's dream, full of names. In it he leaves, his tenement etc. at Hole House to his nephew William, son of his brother Jonathan Jackson of Hazel Head on whom I had done some research as I knew he was a descendant of John Whinfield and Susan (née Casson). (See page 145) This is worthy of a tree:

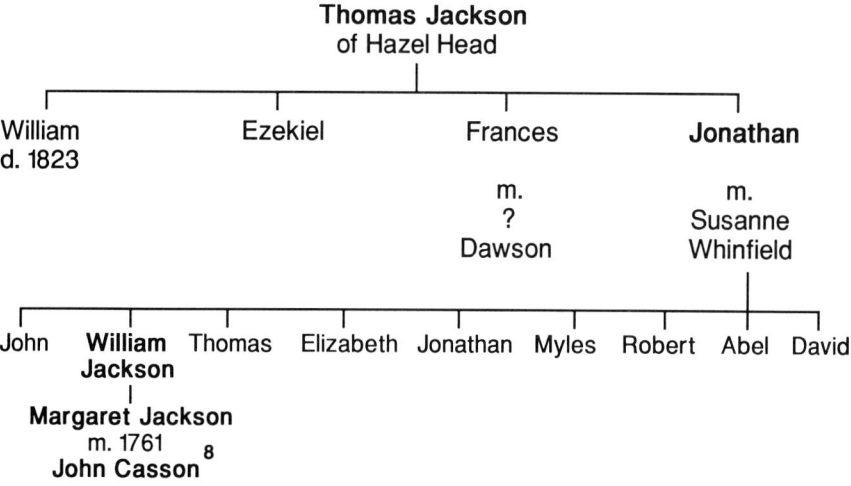

There was another Myles, born the previous year who did not survive, so, as often happened in those days, a later child was given the same name. I do not know who 'my' William married, but I now know from whom he was descended.

Cassons of Kilnbank

The family tree (10), given below uses information from the will of Nicholas Casson, made in 1675. Interestingly, in the will he says *'if my youngest son Roger be alive'* and if not, the legacy is to go to his son, Robert, when he attains the age of twenty-one.

Was Roger ill or was he away?

Nicholas also refers to his son, Joseph, having children, but only names two grandsons, Joseph and Nicholas, without giving their parents names.

Casson - Tree 9

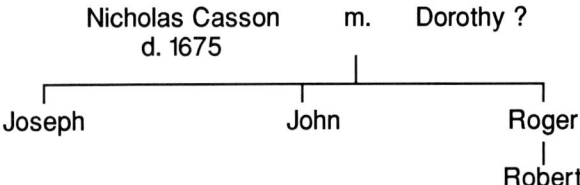

Another interesting will, but later, is that of John Casson of Kilnbank, dyer, proved 29th March 1734, in which he mentions his sister Isabel Thompson and her four daughters, the daughter of his nephew, Thomas Casson who is blind, his god-daughter Mary Casson of Low Herst (T8), and his nephew Russell Casson *'if he comes to demand it'*. I do not whether he did go to demand it, but I do know who he was. Research found him baptised at Egremont in 1704, son of Nicholas who was a steward of the Earl of Egremont. Later, Russell was to be found at Burton, Kendal, where he married in 1725 Elizabeth Chambers.

Was John the dyer the one above? Was Nicholas the grandson?
No matter how hard one tries, to sort all Cassons into families is an impossibility.

I have been unable to construct reliable trees for the Casson family until Joseph[1], born 1719 who is mentioned in his father Robert's will (Tree 7). He married in 1746, Mary Pritt from Stonestar and raised seven children. The Pritts sometimes spelt Pratt or Pirt, were yet another well established family, many branches becoming Baptists.

Casson - Tree 10

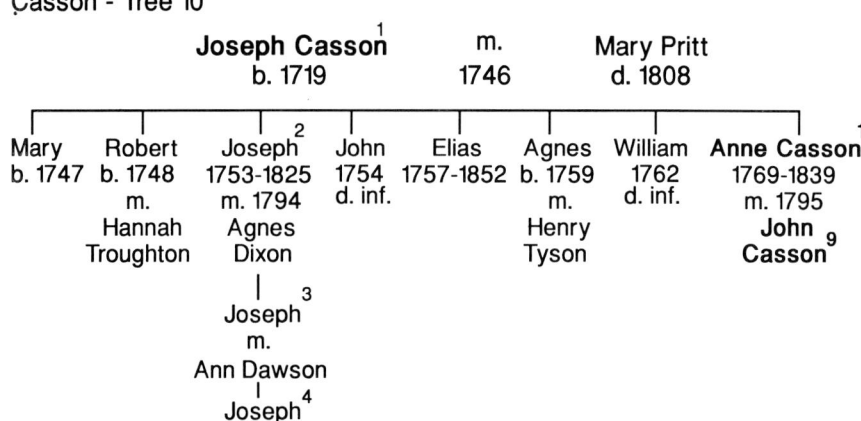

John Casson[8] pre-deceased his father, so Low Herst went to his son John[9] who, in 1795, married Anne Casson, daughter of Joseph Casson[1] of Kilnbank, who was his grandmother's brother. (See Casson trees 7, 8 and 10)

Ann Dawson, who married Joseph Casson[3] was a descendant of the Cassons of Frith Hall, who were to move to Newfield sometime in the 1720s. The manor court roll of 1715 *'held at the house of John Casson de Frith Hall'* which by that time would be an *'ale-house'* so there would be no change of occupation when he moved to Newfield.

I think that, before I go into more details of the Kilnbank and Newfield Cassons, I will go back to the family at Low Hurst (T8) and particularly to the third son of John[6] and Mary, Ferdinando[1]. He appears to have been a miller before he inherited Sella, working the mill near Oak Bank. He married Anne Atkinson of Frith Hall, daughter of Anthony Atkinson and Margaret Croudson whose family has been traced back to the Stanleys of Dale Garth in Eskdale valley. As I said before, the Atkinsons had been around since at least 1510 and from an early date can be traced to Biggardmire, but, like the Jacksons, Cassons and Tysons, spread their large families far and wide, using the same Christian names and so making it difficult to fit many of them into families. As they are my direct ancestors, through their youngest daughter, Margaret, marring William Stephenson[2], I will give the tree. They are a family which is being well researched by various descendants; perhaps we will get a book on them one day.

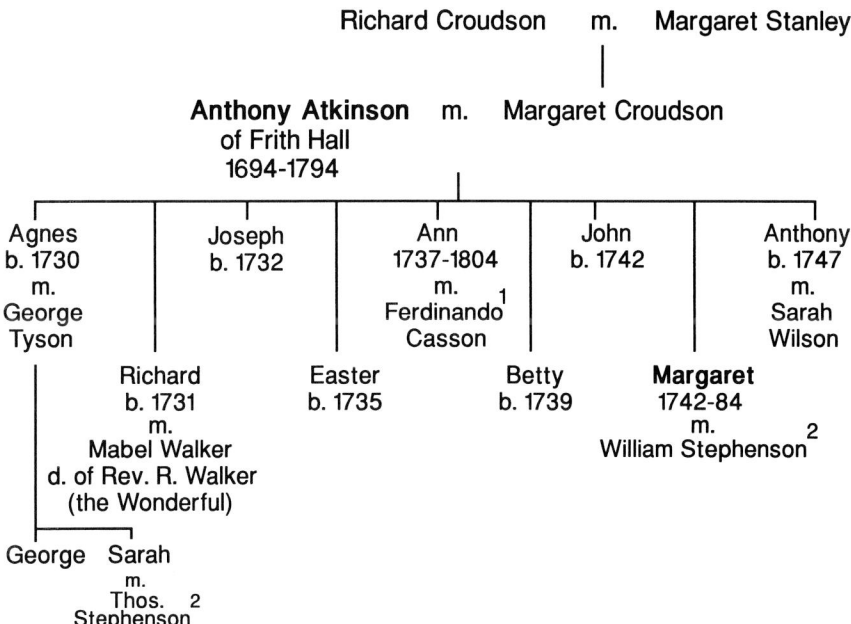

Much research has been carried out into these families. Agnes Atkinson was married and having children while 'my' Margaret was still a schoolgirl. Agnes' son, George, was to marry the daughter of the Vicar of Eskdale and her daughter Sarah, was to marry the Rev. Thomas Stephenson[2], brother of Margaret Atkinson's husband, thus Margaret was both aunt and sister-in-law to Sarah! (see pages 68 and 69) I wonder how often this happened when people had large families.

Richard Atkinson owned much property and land and his will names many nephews and nieces, as does that of his niece, Sarah Stephenson. His widow lived in Liverpool after his death, I think with her sister, as a letter from the Rev. Ferdinando Casson[2] (Tree 12) of Chester speaks of visiting 'Aunt Mab'. (p. 158)

Joseph, I believe, went to America, the others found local spouses. Margaret has been recorded in the Stephenson chapter, so now we turn to Ann and Ferdinando Casson[1] who, as I have said, eventually went to reside at Sella. Their address was given in the register at the baptism of their first two children as Mill House, but none was given for the next two. Nor do I know the date when the Sella tenancies became one.

Back to the Cassons

Casson - Tree 11

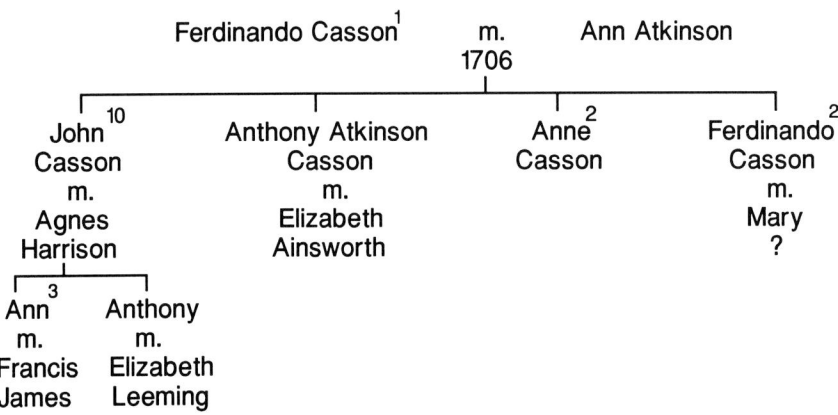

John[10] inherited the Mill from his father and lived at High Herst; whether he owned one of the cottages there is not known. Of his children, Ann[3], born at Torver, married Francis James, miller. (There is an extensive pedigree of the James family by Dr. Boyes, in the CRO, Carlisle) and his youngest son, Anthony, married at Lancaster, Elizabeth Leeming. They lived at Ulverston and were Quakers.

Anthony Atkinson Casson, born in 1770, had his mother's maiden name as a Christian name. This practice became very popular, and continues even to the present day, but this is the earliest example in any of the families I have researched. He married Elizabeth Ainsworth, inherited Sella, and produced one son, John, and one daughter who survived infancy.

John[11], born in 1809, married Jane Dickinson and had a large family which was born over a period of twenty five years between 1828 and 1853. Jane must have had a hard life; she was eventually killed on her way to market.

All the children were educated and all the sons put to a trade. Tradition has it, that John was a hard man ruling his family with a rod of iron. He stipulated that if any of his children left home, they were not to return.

Casson - Tree 12

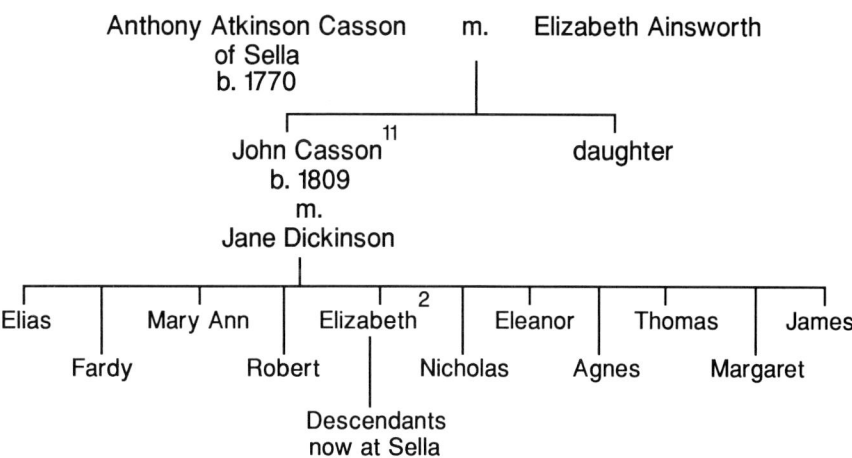

Anthony Atkinson Casson m. Elizabeth Ainsworth
of Sella
b. 1770

John Casson[11]   daughter
b. 1809
m.
Jane Dickinson

Elias | Mary Ann | Elizabeth[2] | Eleanor | Thomas | James
Fardy | Robert | Nicholas | Agnes | Margaret

Descendants
now at Sella

Elias, for a number of years prior to emigrating to Australia in 1851, kept a diary, recording the weather and events of importance that took place in the valley. He married, but died young, leaving a daughter.

In 1854, brothers Fardy, by trade a blacksmith, and Robert, a shoemaker, emigrated to Australia, they eventually went to the goldfields and both died as bachelors, not having made their fortunes.

In 1855, Mary Ann followed her brothers to Australia where she married. She had thirteen children - even more than her mother.

Some years later, Elizabeth[2] also emigrated to Australia, but, for reasons unknown, returned to England. Her father enforced his rule, and his daughter had to live with an aunt until she married. Her descendants today own Sella.

Eleanor was drowned in the Duddon.

Several descendants of Mary Ann's large family have visited the U.K., looking for their roots.

The Rev. Ferdinando Casson[2]

We must now return to Ferdinando Casson[2], born in 1781 (see tree 13), the youngest son of Ferdinando[1] and Ann née Atkinson, who gave him a good education to set him forth in life. He obtained an M.A., probably at Dublin, and went to Chester where he ran a very success-ful school. Later he became a minor Canon of Chester Cathedral. I have not found his marriage to Mary.

Casson - Tree 13

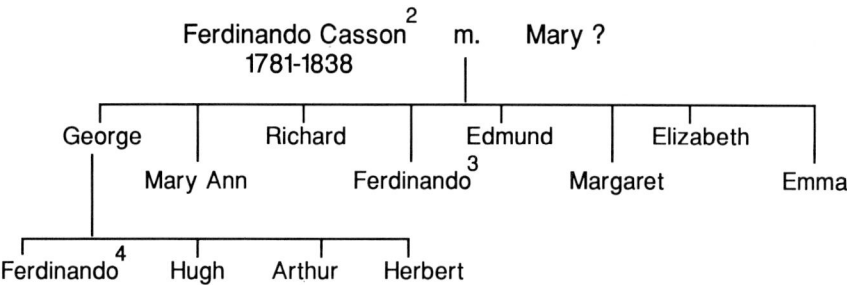

Of their eight children, shown on the above tree, four died young as listed on a Tablet in the South Transept of Chester Cathedral

To the Memory of
Richard, son of the Revd. Ferdinando Casson and Mary his wife
Who died April 10[th.] 1817 aged six years
Also of Edmund who died April 29[th.] 1817 aged two years.
And of Ferdinando who died May [3rd.] 1817 aged four years
Also of Mary Anne their daughter who died April 21[t.] aged seven
years and six months.

This must have been a sad time for the family.

Ferdinando[2] kept in touch with his brother at Sella; in a letter he wrote, he spoke about salving his sheep, going to see Aunt Mab at Liverpool, and taking the opportunity of sending this letter with Elias who was coming home. At the time of seeing this letter, I had no idea who Elias was, but when I did find him he was from Kilnbank!

Of their surviving children, George followed his father and took Holy Orders. He was educated at Oxford, receiving a B.A. in 1831 and an M.A. in 1834. He was Vicar of Old in Northamptonshire, from 1842 until 1870. I have visited this church, but the only mention of him is a small tablet, next to the organ, in memory of his first wife who had died young.

However, research found that he had four sons, Ferdinando[4], Hugh, Arthur and Herbert. Three of these died without issue.

Ferdinando[4] (1864-1900) was killed in the Boer War.

Hugh, born in 1866, rose to be a Brigadier General.

Arthur was drowned.

Herbert was with the Indian Civil Service; he married in 1897 and had one daughter.

These are grandsons that the Rev. Ferdinando would have been proud of.

In 1931, Herbert and his daughter, both living at Tyn-y-coed, Arthog, Wales, tried to find their roots. They were interested in a Casson Coat of Arms, which several branches of the family used but they were unsuccessful in trying to prove it at the College of Heralds.

Of Ferdinando[2]'s daughters I know nothing, they were still single when their mother's will was proved in 1847.

Ferdinando Casson[2] died in 1838, leaving an estate worth £25,000 - not bad for the youngest son who was just given a good education to set him forth in life!

The following tablet was erected in the Nave of Chester Cathedral but some years ago after being cleaned was moved to another location.

In Honorable Rememberance of
The Reverent Ferdinando Casson M.A.
One of the Minor Canon of the Cathedral Church and many years
Both a teacher and an example to a large Portion of the
surrounding youth of piety towards God.
Devoted attachment to the constitution of his Country and the
Constant exercise of every Christian Virtue
This Monument is Erected
By his grateful and affectionate pupils.
He died March 22[nd.] 1838 Aged 56 years

Thus the Casson name died out at Sella.

Cassons of Frith Hall and Newfield

Frith Hall, thought to have been built as a hunting lodge for the Hudlestons, is now, sadly, a ruin. It must have been an impressive place commanding a fine view of the valley. I think it is the 'New Hall' referred to in the Manor Court Rolls. The first reference I have of its present name is in 1715. If this is right, Old Hall, now also a ruin must be older. There has been speculation that the earliest church was somewhere in that vicinity and The Rev. Peter Chamberlaine, who owed money to Nicholas Casson[1] (Tree 1), was admitted to the tenancy of Brackenthwaite around that time. In those long gone days, these dwellings were on the main trade route, from or to Ravenglass via Birkermoor, past Crosbythwaite, Baskell, Pykeside, Biggartmire and Brackenthwaite, making its way to Rowfold Bridge either via Logan Beck or Frith Hall and hence over the Dunnerdale tops and so to Hawkshead or Kendal.

At the general fine of 1688, John Casson was admitted to half a tenement at Cattholes and in the margin was written *'Robert Casson by purchase.'* Was this Robert the father of John?

The next list of fines is 1720 when John Casson was admitted to five tenements which included Cattholes and Pykeside, surely one of the unnamed ones was Frith Hall. John Casson[12] and his wife Ann, of Frith Hall had their daughter Agnes baptised in 1718, followed in 1721 by son Robert, another son John in 1722, a daughter Ann in 1726 and a son William in 1729. These last three died in infancy. That John called his first son Robert, makes one think that the Robert first mentioned, was his father. A Robert Casson of Frith Hall died 1707 followed by a widow Agnes of the same place in 1736, but as there are no wills, the relationship has not been proved.

It is more difficult to establish which branch of the Cassons were at Frith Hall, it is possible they were the same as those at Panel Holme as in 1727, John of Panel Holme was presented to the Court *'for letting his tenement at Whinfield Ground to John Jackson without a licence from the Lord'* (there was more than one tenement there). With this John owning property so close it gets more confusing. It makes one wonder whether, in those days people dealt in property, received it as an inheritance or bought it. In 1725 there is a baptism of John, son of John Casson of Whinfield Ground, it is possible that the property was bought for this son?

John[12] and Ann Casson took over Newfield from the Flemings. Ann died in 1746 and John a few years later both are buried at Ulpha. I have been unable to find a will.

Newfield

Casson - Tree 14

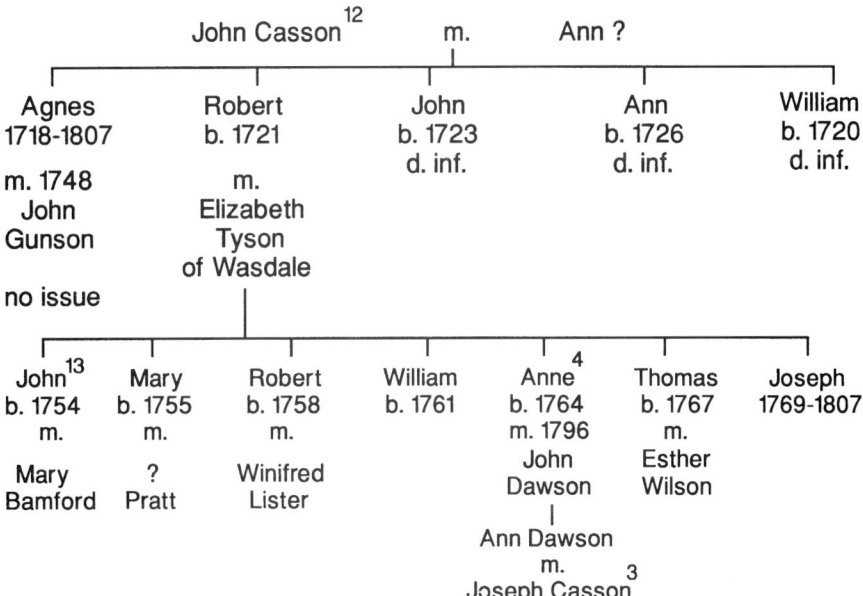

John Casson[12]   m.   Ann ?

| Agnes 1718-1807 | Robert b. 1721 | John b. 1723 d. inf. | Ann b. 1726 d. inf. | William b. 1720 d. inf. |

Agnes 1718-1807
m. 1748
John
Gunson
no issue

Robert b. 1721
m.
Elizabeth
Tyson
of Wasdale

| John[13] b. 1754 m. Mary Bamford | Mary b. 1755 m. ? Pratt | Robert b. 1758 m. Winifred Lister | William b. 1761 | Anne[4] b. 1764 m. 1796 John Dawson | Thomas b. 1767 m. Esther Wilson | Joseph 1769-1807 |

Ann Dawson
m.
Joseph Casson[3]

Agnes Casson, their daughter, (1717-1807), died after her husband, John Gunson. Her inventory is interesting, containing items not mentioned in earlier ones studied, so giving further insight into the possessions of people living almost three hundred years ago. Items mentioned were as follows

'One large looking-glass, one corner cupboard, my best round table, one silver pint and one tea caddy.'

At this period, around the time of the Napoleonic Wars, there was a lot of movement, and the Casson family were no exception. Of the large family of Robert Casson (born 1721), John[13] (1754) who married Mary Bamford, a granddaughter of the Revd. Robert (Wonderful) Walker, was the only son to stay in the Valley.

Two other sons, William, born 1761 and Thomas, (1767) moved to Festiniog in Wales, where they started the famous slate quarries. Thomas had married Esther Wilson, another grand-daughter of the Rev. Robert Walker. The brothers rode on horseback to Wales, with Esther riding pillion behind her husband. More details of this family and their renowned descendants can be read in the book *'Lewis and Sybil'* by the late John Casson, with whom I corresponded some years ago, when he gave me permission to quote from this book, in which he said that, during the 1745 uprising, The Revd Wonderful Walker hid his grandfather clock in a quarry on Walna Scar! This same clock was then still in the Casson family having been to Australia and back to the U.K.

For my readers who may not be familiar with the The Revd Robert Walker, he was born at Undercragg, Seathwaite, the youngest of a large family, he married Anne Tyson of Loweswater at Dean. His career as a teacher, took him to Gosforth and Loweswater and finally back to Seathwaite to be the curate. He remained there for sixty-six years. He wove as he taught the children in the Church, wrote many of his parishioners' wills, farmed his glebe, gave soup to his flock, many of whom came a long distance on a Sunday. He and his wife had a large family who were all educated. His stipend was £5 a year, later to rise to £10. When he died he left the remarkable sum of £2,000 thus earning him the title of 'The Wonderful'. He was buried on June 28th. 1802 *'in the 93rd. year of his age.'* Anne predeceased him and was buried on February 1st. 1800 also in her ninety-third year. There is a note in the Church register which reads, after giving the length of his curacy, *'He was a man singular for his Temperance, Industry and Integrity'.* Wordsworth knew and wrote about him.

Seathwaite Church

To return to the children of Robert Casson and his wife Elizabeth Tyson, (Tree 14). Their son, Robert, born in 1758, was a glazier who was living at Croscanonby when, in 1787, he married Winifred Lister at Holy Trinity Church, Whitehaven. The youngest of his brothers was living at 'Newbiggin' when he died; which one I do not know as there were several. Of his sisters, Mary married someone named Pratt and Anne[4] married John Dawson. John and Anne produced a daughter, also Ann, who brought us back to Cassons by marrying Joseph Casson[3] of Kilnbank (Tree 11). Joseph[4], their eldest son, had issue but all died without leaving a male heir, so yet another branch of the Casson family died out.

Joseph Casson[3] and his wife Ann née Dawson, with their grandson.

Back to Low Hurst

Casson - Tree 15

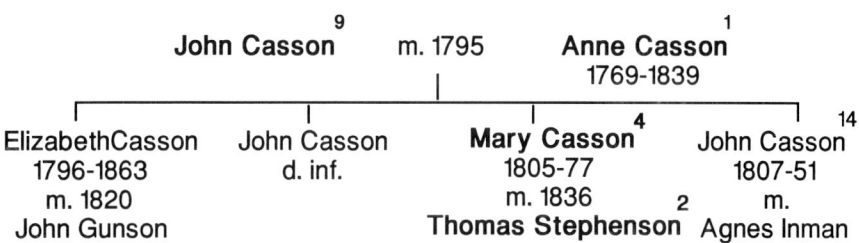

John Casson[9]   m. 1795   Anne Casson[1]
                                 1769-1839

ElizabethCasson	John Casson	Mary Casson[4]	John Casson[14]
1796-1863	d. inf.	1805-77	1807-51
m. 1820		m. 1836 [2]	m.
John Gunson		Thomas Stephenson	Agnes Inman

John[14] died without issue so that the property was divided between my great-grandmother and her sister Elizabeth Gunson. This was the end of the Casson name at Low Hurst. The last mention in the registers of a Casson of Newfield, is the marriage, in 1818, of Agnes Casson a minor aged 19 to Isaac Satterthwaite. There were still families of Cassons in Hall Dunnerdale whose trees I have not recorded.

Elizabeth Gunson's grandson was the benefactor who built the alms-houses now known as Gunsons Cottages in Ulpha. When first built, they were intended for the old and poor who had lived or worked in the valley, the tenants paid no rent and received ten shillings a week. They each had a garden in which to produce vegetables.

To sum up the Cassons: the trees I have given are families I have researched in depth, there are many more. Elias Casson (Tree 11) was an Officer of Customs and Excise and was stationed at Chester, he is mentioned in the Rev. Ferdinado[2]'s letter. Elias died in 1852, at the age of ninety-five, a bachelor, leaving the interest of his money first to one niece, and after her day, to another niece. Both nieces lived into their nineties, and the money then went to the children of his brothers and sisters. Finally, in 1899, the will was settled. There were nine divisions; I have a copy of the one in which my father received less than one pound, but the settlement gives all his Casson relatives and I have seen another one of them in which there were so many descendants they only received five shillings and a few pence apiece, but wonderful documents for Family History. From these nine divisions, had I been able to trace them all, would have revealed, I am sure, over a hundred cousins or second cousins!

Still with Tree 11, Joseph Casson[3], had a son, Joseph[4], who lived to the age of ninety-seven but, in his later years, became blind. This is the second incidence of blindness of a Casson connected with Kilnbank (see page 153) Today, the medical profession often ask patients to do their family tree to see if they can trace a disease as being hereditary. This happened in my own family, leading to a family reunion.

Cassons could be found in groups as far north as Workington and Whitehaven, with the occasional family in other villages. However, in the 17th and 18th. centuries, the biggest concentration was in south Cumberland and the Furness area of north Lancashire. There were also some in the Cartmel area. Where did they originate from? The 'son' on the end of the name suggests a Norse origin. There have been suggestions they could have come from the village of Casson in France, but one thing is certain, they were in the valley in 1510 and the majority of them lived long lives.

Joseph Casson in the kitchen at Kilnbank.

PART 5 MISCELLANEA

Of the many other families in the Duddon Valley with whom I am connected, I will mention just two.

Tysons

I can say with certainty that ninety nine percent, if not all the families already mentioned have a Tyson in their family tree, as this name was found in Westmorland, Cumberland and North Lancashire. When I was researching the Hird family I got back to Edward Tyson who married Dorothy Nicholson, but no further as there were six Edward Tysons having children baptised at the same period and even though the vicar gave the address I have not been able to find his parents. In fact I have come to a dead end on most of my Tyson lines so I thought some Local Social History would be the best way to acknowledge them.

In the Duddon Valley, the Tyson country was above the church, as were the Walkers and Dawsons, the Tysons continuing right up to Black Hall and Gaitscall on the Cumberland side of the river and ending on the Lancashire side at Cockley Beck, which must have always been a busy place. As it is the first dwelling encountered after travelling from Eskdale via Hardknott or from Langdale via Wrynose Pass, it would always be a calling place for travellers, and whichever way they had come they would have had a hilly journey.

In the late 1800s visitors, other than those travelling through work or trade, began to discover the valley. Mr. and Mrs. Tyson of Cockley Beck, kept a Visitors Book which is, in itself, a chapter of history. On the front page is written *'John Tyson   Visitors Book'* then, on the opposite page in different but extremely good hand writing *'Notice to Visitors. You are particularly requested to abstain from defacing this Visitors book, Or writing any nonsense therin Signed Baron Trench 2 Sept. 1871'* Whoever he was, he had gone through the book adding remarks to other visitors entries and even adding pictures (see p. 168). The type of person who did not win any admiration; but there were others, too, who referred to their host as 'Tyson', omitting the Mister, an attitude adopted in those days by the town folk, who considered themselves so much cleverer and more sophisticated than country folk.

The first entry, however is dated Sept. 14[th.] 1869 and reads - *'Very much pleased with the kindness of Mrs Tyson, where I stayed all night'.* Signed: Mrs. Hird Langdale. There were, however, those better mannered than the 'baron', who appreciated what their host gave

Thornbury Park

These are barrows

These are rocks

View from Thornbury house as seen on a very wet day in September

This is a view at Thorne house Clevedon Park as it appeared in the year 1851. previous to the alteration. It is taken from an ancient engraving in the British Museum.

31 August 1871 with us at

Capt. ....
Mr. A. Freeman — do.
Bertie Craven — to —
Walter Craven — to —

Capt. & Mrs Villiers Kimbold Cook Greenwich Hospital
Edward J. Cook Win. Coll.

Sept 7. Patison 3 St Fort. St. London S.C.
do. do.
W. A. Morris do.
H. J. Moston 7 Phillips Park Upp. [Brook]

Sept 3 1871. Mr & Mrs. H. Thomson of Orrington
arrived here last night, also a Mr a Caterpiller...
Harold Frere...

them and his wealth of knowledge. In 1874, Sandy Kent of Oldham and companion described their walk of twelve miles and getting caught in the rain continued *'when we reached Tyson's house we were very hospitably dealt with, being replenished with a first Class tea served up in a most admirable manner by Mrs Tyson and you can judge for your selves as to the part we played at the table, one eating a whole spread* (buttered) *loaf, twelve milk biscuits and a tasty bit of parkin covered with jam for desert, after which we got squatted round a bright blazing fire of wood and turf* (peat) *with Mr Tyson's Mountain Coats and boots on. Ours being taken off to get dried for morning and after a pleasant half an hour chat about the mountains and the life they lead we were conducted to our sleeping apartments.'* Next morning, before breakfast, they went for a walk returning to *'Cream, butter, ham, eggs, etc which was un-rivalled for excellence'* they then started on their way over Wrynose for Ambleside.

Reading many of these comments, one gets the impression that these tourists were greatly surprised at the standard of food and the accommodation. I have no doubt the food would be served on lovely china plates, the valley folks had plenty. [At a sale in the early 1920s, attended by dealers from a wide area, handle-less cups and saucers, the first of their kind, and single plates, were bringing huge sums of money.] On Sept. 7$^{th.}$ 1875 the book shows a large party calling, five ladies and five gentlemen whose address was given as Eccleston Square, London, and underneath was written *'from the Home Secretary's household'* they were accompanied by Mr & Mrs Dawson of Broughton-in-Furness and Mr. Jackson of Liverpool. Was this a Staff outing? The Home Secretary could well have been staying with Sir R.A. Cross G.C.B., M.P. whose residence was Eccle Riggs.

By then, the valley was becoming well known, callers coming from all parts of the British Isles and from abroad. A party of walkers, en route from Buttermere via Wasdale to Ambleside, included a gentleman from Jersey and one from Edinburgh; summer brought them from the Lancashire and Yorkshire towns. Some called for meals, others for accomodation and others, just for a drink, which was usually milk as Messrs Sunduis Smith and Thomas Wilkinson recorded, *'Milk Excellent'* adding that, on they previous day, they had lost their way in dense fog at the top of Scawfell Pike.

1898 saw more organised walks, as, in May, Messrs Garnet, Fidler, Atkinson, Cartner, Miller and Simpson, all of the *'Egremont Touring Club'* called; next, their neighbours the *'Eskdale Touring Club'*, called on their way back from Bowness and Langdale Gala and Sports. In that same year, Peter Hill of Scotland was the first to mention the latest form of recreation *'Dear fellow cyclists never bring your Bikes this way'*

Many of these walkers were ladies who must have been tough to have undertaken such strenuous walks in heavy cumbersome dresses.

I will finish this with an entry of July 1871 giving advice which still applies today. *'One John Fox had inadvertently given Mr. Tyson a great deal of trouble, but Mr. T. took it it all in very good part and J.F. takes leave very thankful to have made the acquaintance of so good kind and true Christian a person as Mr. Tyson. J.F. lost his way coming from the top of Coniston Old Man - in addition he lost much time from a continuous attack by two hawks and a buzzard. He records his experience as a warning to others not to go alone without a map or a stick. Mrs Tyson really resuscitated vital energy which was well nigh exhausted.'*

That the population moved around can be seen by the marriage bond dated 1753 of John Tyson of Christcliff, in Eskdale, skinner, aged 28 years and Elizabeth Wilson of Brotherilkeld (or Butterilket) aged 22 years of the parish of Millom (but actually in the Eskdale Valley) spinster, the marriage to take place at Hawkshead, and the Bondsman was John Jackson, another skinner, from Monk Coniston which was also in the parish of Hawkshead

Just another Tyson snippet: in 1719 there was a dispute as to who was responsible for repairing a yate or gate at Grassguards and as it went to the court, various people were asked to make dispositions, amongst these was one from Thomas Tyson, of the parish of Hawkshead, who describes himself as *'One of the People called Quakers'* and goes on to say that, about forty years since, his father, another Thomas Tyson, was a hind to Wm. Askew Gent. of Grassguards etc. giving us a date long before any surviving registers and a hint he may have been the ancestor of Hugh Tyson (page 83). There was a lot of movement over the passes between what I call 'the top of the valleys folk', or perhaps it would be more clear if I said from the top of the parishes whose boundaries all met at the Three Shire Stone, and also with Hawkshead, the latter particularly for Religious purposes.

Wilsons

Again, the name is connected by marriage with most families in all three counties and further afield, so I shall give a short history of those from Brotherilkeld and Ulpha. In 1689, John Wilson of Brotherilkeld made his will, mentioning sons, Edward and John and daughters, Joyce and Jennet Wilson and Elizabeth, wife of George Brocklebank. This will was proved in April 1690. His wife, Agnes, was to bring up the children who were minors, John, Joyce and Jennet. His estate was valued at £165.3s.6d and he owed £45.

In 1689, Edward Wilson, a bachelor, made his will, full of names, including John Wilson but does not give any relationship. It was proved in April 1694 by his sister Joyce Tyson; his estate was £100.6.4d. This Edward would be John's son. Both died rich men.

In 1728, another Edward Wilson made his will in November and died the following month. He was even richer leaving £292.10s. Again another example of leaving money *'unto my son Benjamin Wilson Forty pounds upon condition that he comes personally himself to receive it and give my Excecutor a Lawful Discharge'*

His tree is below.

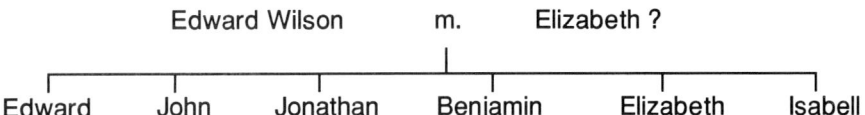

```
          Edward Wilson      m.      Elizabeth ?
                              |
   ┌──────────┬──────────┬──────────┬──────────┬──────────┐
 Edward     John    Jonathan   Benjamin   Elizabeth    Isabell
```

The eldest son, Edward, will be the one who came to Ulpha to the Law and married Thomasina Coulthred of Hawkshead, daughter of a Baptist Minister and so the Baptist religion came to the valley. Their family all married local girls, with the exception of John.

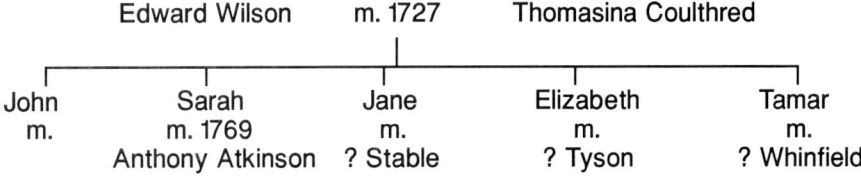

```
          Edward Wilson    m. 1727    Thomasina Coulthred
                              |
   ┌──────────┬──────────┬──────────┬──────────┬──────────┐
  John      Sarah       Jane      Elizabeth     Tamar
   m.      m. 1769       m.          m.           m.
        Anthony Atkinson  ? Stable   ? Tyson   ? Whinfield
```

Edward, however died at Newfield, Seathwaite. Their descendants spread to Langdale, Furness and Nether Wasdale and are mentioned in many deeds of property in a wide area. Why they became Baptists I do not know, but I do know that, in 1807, at Lancaster Quarter Sessions, they applied to have the Law registered as a place of worship.

'These are to certify that at the general Quarter Sessions of the Peace held at Lancaster in and for the said County the 26th. Day of April in the Fortyeighth Year of King George the Thirds reign A house the property and occupied by John Wilson situated at the Law in the Chapelry of Ulpha within the Dioces of Chester was duly registered as a Place of Religious Worship for Protestant Dissenters.'

How long the place served as such I do not know, but I have notes of worshippers being dipped in 'Susannah's Dub'. I hope it was in summer as the Duddon water can be very cold!

I was privileged to look at some of the Wilson private papers and was surprised to see that in 1727 one of the Wilson brothers had a shop in Whitehaven and fifty-odd years later, in April 1783, John Wilson, son of John Wilson of Law in the parish of Millom, aged 19 years was apprenticed to Fletcher and Sutherland to learn the art of Seamanship. They certainly moved around.

In John senior's will, proved in 1809, he makes no mention of son John, so one is inclined to think that he must have died. One interesting item in the will is the mention of coppiced wood, a valuable source of income. It was cut down every fifteen years and sold for the making of bobbins and charcoal.

There are many more families, but I will leave them for others to record. If all the descendants of those mentioned in this book could be traced I would indeed be surrounded by a forest of cousins of some degree !

Clergy mentioned in the text.

As you will have read, a number of clergy are mentioned in this book. Over the years, I have collected information, with the help of the late C. Roy Hudleston, who collated a large index of 'Northern Parsons'. Whenever I visited a churchyard, it was a 'must' to find a headstone recording one which would help to swell his collection. He, in turn, always gave me any information he had concerning any parsons I found amongst my ancestors. His index can be seen in the Dept. of Palaeography at Durham University.

The following are some details of my kin;

The Revd Nicholas Casson[5], 1682-1748
    b. Dunnerdale; Vicar of South Clifton, Notts.

The Revd Ferdinando Casson[2] M.A. 1772-1838
    b. Dunnerdale; Minor canon, Chester Cathedral.

The Revd George Casson (son of the above)
    b. Chester; Vicar of Old, Northants.

The Revd. John Jackson 1717-
    b. Ulpha; educated St. Bees School & Glasgow University.
    Vicar of Underbarrow.

The Revd. Christopher Moor B.A.
    born Irton, Cumberland; assistant master at Rugby School.

The Revd. Robert Coalbank
    b. Nether Wasdale; Clerk of the Parish of Plaitford, Wilts 1835;
    at Frisky on the Wreak, Leics. 1838;
    at Snedshell, Shiffnal in 1847.

The Revd Samuel Sherwen 1790-1860
    b. Seascale How, Gosforth; Deacon, Chester 1813;
    curate of Embleton; Usher at Cockermouth Grammar School;
    Officiating Minister at Dean 1815 and Minister there until his
    death.
    Said to have walked from Cumberland to Chester.

The Revd. Robert Stephenson d. 1747, Irton.
    b. Irton; Curate of Corney; vicar of Innes.

The Revd Daniel Stephenson 1711-78
    b. Ulpha; Curate of Thwaites Nr. Millom.

The Revd. Thomas Stephenson[2] 1759-1820
    b. Ulpha; Curate of Whitechapel, Goosnargh 1796-1808;
    Curate, Lund 1818-20 and curate at Kirkham; Temporary Master of
    Kirkham Grammar School. Obit (1820) Preston Chronicle.
    Left estate £3,000. His widow, Sarah, died Eskdale.

Revd. Isaac Tyson, 1766-1820 of Wath, Cleator
    (eldest s. of Jacob Tyson and Jane Stephenson, of Crosbythwaite,
    Ulpha)
    Ordained Deacon, York 1790, Priested York 1792;
    Assisitant Curate at Flecton 1790-92.
    Curate at Harewood and Chaplain to the Lascelles Family 1792;
    Vicar of Hemingbrough and vicar of Adlingfleet 1794-1820.

Revd. Edwin Colman Tyson 1795-1863 (?) (eldest son of the above)
    In Holy orders; held no cure, lived Wakefield until 1854,
    then Milburn nr. Penrith. d. Lazonby.

Revd. Milnes Tyson 1800-60 (second s. to the above Isaac).
    Curate of Wark on Tyne 1841-2.

Revd. William Daniel Tyson 1804-65
    (youngest son of of the above Isaac)
    Curate of Hibaldston, Lincs 1846-51;
    Curate of Barrow, Derby 1853-6,
    curate of Doulting, Somerset 1856-8 and of Milburn, west. 1858-65.

It is interesting to note the distances travelled by some of these men
of the cloth; the earlier ones like Nicholas and Ferdinando Casson and
Isaac Tyson, would have travelled by coach, horseback or even on
foot, over roads which left much to be desired, bumps, potholes and
overhanging trees, not to mention the danger of highwaymen.

Memories

I have been blessed with two things, a good number of bonus years over life's allotted span and a good memory. I was fortunate to be brought up in an age, now sadly gone, when, *'children should be seen and not heard'*; however, we *were* allowed to listen and so learned an awful lot! I never found it boring, I studied people, and discovered who was genuine, and who wasn't. As long as you didn't show too much interest, you heard all the tasty bits of scandal, but if you did show even the slightest bit of interest, well, *'little pigs have big ears'* and the adults changed the subject!

As my father was an invalid, we lived in the cottage of the family home of Moorhouse, so most of my childhood was spent on the farm. It wasn't a big farm like those of today, but the work was hard. There were no tractors, work was done manually, with horses for ploughing, mowing, reaping and 'mucking the fields' (adding manure). Hay and corn were loaded on carts and taken to the barns, and for special occasions and outings there was a horse and trap to convey people.

There never seemed to be a slack season, as, in winter, wall gaps were mended, cowhouses whitewashed and implements mended. Most ploughing was done in spring, the corn sown, the potatoes set, turnips and mangold-wurzels sown, always working on the rotation system. My uncle had a saying 'March dust is worth a guinea an ounce', meaning that the winds were welcome to dry the soil so that these jobs could be done.

For the hill farmers, the first lambs appeared about mid April, as did the chickens. It was a lovely time for children; we were taught from an early age, how to feed the lambs that had lost their mothers and feed the chicks, making sure they were secure from predators.

Summer was perhaps the busiest time of the year, especially for the women, who not only had to feed the extra hands that came to help with the clipping and haytime, they also had to lend a hand in the fields as well as dealing with the soft fruit, picking it and making jam. One task for the farmer was thinning the turnips (swedes), this was done on knees, wrapped round with sacking, crawling between the rows - a very tedious job. In the 20's and 30's, men on the dole would walk out from the towns at daybreak to do this on nearby farms, for 6d a row. They finished before 7.00 pm in case they were caught, perhaps earning half a crown a day which supplemented their small allowance.

August was the month when family from away visited and the houses were bulging. I loved it. Big gatherings of aunts, uncles, cousins and friends, some going off walking, some fishing and on the 'Glorious Twelfth', grouse shooting. On Sunday afternoons they all went to the little Weslyan Chapel, which was only open in the summer months, the singing was wonderful. The month went too quickly.

Autumn, the time to gather the bracken for winter bedding for the animals, get the peats, lift the root crops and potatoes and put them into clamps, gather the fruit and go into the woods to collect the hazel nuts. For the farmers, by October the sheep would have been sorted and the hogs ready to be taken to their winter quarters, onto low lying farms. This is still done, but now they are conveyed by cattle trucks; in those days, the farmer walked them, travelling many miles. Surplus sheep were taken to the auction and sold. In the 1920's and 30's, farming was very bad; many young people, who were trying to get established, failed and their property had to be sold. Wool, like today, was at a very low price.

In winter, we always seemed to have snow and frost. The men would manure the fields. All farms had a midden, and the manure was taken in a cart, deposited in small heaps on the ground and spread with a fork. The cattle and horses would all be inside, they

were let out morning and evening every day to go to the stream for a drink. This was the time for farm repairs, the men going up the fells to mend wall gaps would take their dinner with them. Gates had to be mended, ditches cleaned out, hedges trimmed and as I said before the buildings whitewashed.

Christmas was a happy time. The Christmas cakes and puddings were made weeks before, and later the mince pies and the sweet pie, (made from diced mutton with dried fruit soaked in rum and covered with puff pastry). The rum butter was made and put in it's special china bowl. Meanwhile, the goose was fattening.

Earlier in the month there would be Whist Drives, with poultry and bottles of whisky for prizes, and then at Christmas, there would be 'Nap' parties. I always thought that this was a Cumbrian game, until recently, when I read about a Polish family, who, on an emigrant ship, *'after prayers played ha'penny nap'.* This is a card game which most men and some women played and the stakes were high. There were many card games, but at home, we usually played for nuts. On New Year's Eve there was what was know as 'The Turkey Hop'. This was a whist drive and dance which included a supper. I was almost fourteen before I was allowed to go, and, having been well trained to play whist, I was thrilled to win the one of the minor prizes, a pound tin of coffee!

Girls played in 'baby houses', the house being a selected corner far away from the main house, here we had broken pots, old pans and anything we could find in the rubbish heap, and we played games of pretend, baking day, washing day, cleaning day, which in autumn was removing leaves. Cakes were made out of mud, and when available, iced with lime.

I must have learned to knit and crochet at a very early age as I don't remember being taught. I seem always to have been making something. Reading too, I can remember laying the local paper on the floor and trying to read that. (I still read them when I visit the Record Offices). I have never made a patchwork quilt, but I remember visiting a house where a lady was making one, it was evening and the only light she had was a candle. Oil lamps were usually only hanging in the living room and sometimes small ones elsewhere but you always went to bed by candle light.

A wonderful piece of machinery was the separator, for extracting the cream from the milk. It was a work of art putting it together and a work of arm power turning the handle to do the job. Likewise, once a week the butter had to be made, churning again by hand, in summer it took ages, round and round sometimes for an hour, but the delicious butter in the end was worth it. When it came out of the churn it had to be worked to get the last drops of milk out, salted, weighed into pounds and half pounds, made into blocks with 'butter pats', marked with your own mark, wrapped in greaseproof paper and kept cool until market day, no fridges, just the cold slabs in the pantry.

Most farmers kept two pigs, one was killed before Christmas and one about February. Pig-killing day was very busy. First the fire under the boiler, or settpot as it was often called, had to be lit to ensure there was plenty of boiling water to help scrape the bristles off. The man who killed the pig arrived shortly after milking time, and it was late afternoon when he had finished, and the carcass was hanging up, the skins cleaned for the sausages and the belly to be made into a pie. The housewife would make the black pudding in a tin. Very few butchers can make them today, although there is one in Broughton-in-Furness who makes a good attempt. Next day, the hams, flitches, and shoulders would be salted, the lard made, spare parts cut up and some given to neighbours, sausages made and roast pork for dinner. Legs of mutton were also salted and hung up to dry, a joint of this boiled with cabbage is another delicacy now long gone.

Most people attended church, either in the morning or evening. Many whist drives and dances raised money for the church upkeep.

In those days there were two schools, one at Seathwaite and the other, although in Dunnerdale, was known as Ulpha School. Regrettably, both are now closed and the children taken to Broughton. I cannot speak too highly of the education I received at Ulpha School, the Head Master, Mr. J. H. Broadbent, was a man of vision, he taught, in the latter years of his career, children of all ages. There was a part time lady who came two days a week to teach the girls sewing and cookery, while he taught the boys woodwork. It was one of the first schools to introduce gardening, which again he taught; from the crops produced, the girls, in their cookery lessons in the wintertime, made soups, which all the scholars had at lunch time. This was a welcome change from the jam sandwiches and piece of cake which was the staple lunch, 'What would you like on your sandwich?' was a question which never arose - we all had jam! The meal was washed down with a drink of cold water, or you could take some tea or cocoa in a little tin and make a hot drink.

Ulpha school

There were seasons for games, skipping, hopscotch, whip-and-top, hare-and-hounds, round games, like 'The Farmer's in his Den', when you sang a song to accompany it and, of course, hide and seek. In summer we played in the streams catching minnows with our hands. What happy days! Even so, children aren't perfect, and one day, at dinner time, the hounds came in full cry - the temptation was too great - we played truant and followed them!

Mr Broadbent possessed a cabinet gramophone; every now and again he got the boys to carry it into the classroom and he played us classical music, pointing out the instruments, thus my love of the classics was born.

He would take us on nature walks, naming the trees and flowers, and on Empire Day, if it was fine, to the top of Yew Barrow and point out landmarks. Another time, we went around a lot of pasture land, looking for signs of previous cultivation. I often wondered, during WW2, if such information was used by the government. Mr. Broadbent was a truly remarkable man.

There were very few motor cars in the 1920's, we could walk in the middle of the road in safety. We children wore clogs and hand-knitted stockings, which kept our feet warm, and, when it was raining, our legs were covered with gaiters, that were buttoned up the side using a button hook.

I remember seeing my first aeroplane, I stood still for ages afterwards, hoping it would come back!

Birks Bridge, Duddon Valley

CONCLUSION

I have taken my readers through many centuries. I am proud of my Cumbrian ancestors, and do not like to see them belittled. Those who had gone long before the times of which I have written, were *not,* as some writers describe them, 'savages'; look at the stone circles they erected, the stepping stones that they placed and the bridges they built which have survived hundreds, if not thousands, of years. These are the work of highly intelligent men from whom we are descended.

M.M.R.
9th. March, 2000

INDEX OF PEOPLE

INDEX OF PLACES